101 THINGS
TO DO WITH
YOUR CAR

101 THINGS
TO DO WITH
YOUR CAR

TAB BOOKS Inc.

Blue Ridge Summit, PA 17214

FIRST EDITION

FIRST PRINTING

Copyright © 1985 by TAB BOOKS Inc.

Printed in the United States of America

Reproduction or publication of the content in any manner, without express
permission of the publisher, is prohibited. No liability is assumed with respect to
the use of the information herein.

Library of Congress Cataloging in Publication Data

Main entry under title:

101 things to do with your car.

    Excerpts from articles originally published in
School shop magazine, 1951-1961.
    Includes index.
    1. Automobile engineering—Study and teaching.
2. Automobile engineering—Laboratory manuals.
I. School shop. II. Title: One hundred one things to
do with your car. III. Title. One hundred and one
things to do with your car.
TL156.A12   1985   629.2'3'078   85-22271
ISBN 0-8306-0173-2
ISBN 0-8306-2073-7 (pbk.)

Contents

Your Own Pickup Truck—Pickup Truck Box Cover—Special Painting Techniques—Trailer Winch—Auto Ramp—Welding Bench

101 THINGS
TO DO WITH
YOUR CAR

Introduction

Do-it-yourself auto enthusiasts can save money and gain satisfaction from investing time and effort in a worthwhile hobby. In this book, you will find discussions of automotive repairs, maintenance techniques, and automotive projects of general interest to beginning hobbyists and some things for more advanced enthusiasts. There are sections covering do-it-yourself diagnosis, using shop tools, and working on engines and electrical systems. There is also information on automotive maintenance and advanced shop work and equipment.

All of the outstanding projects in this book have been made available by the editors of *School Shop* magazine, the how-to-do-it publication that has printed articles relating to industrial and technical education since 1941. Without their efforts and cooperation, this book would not be possible.

Chapter 1

Do-It-Yourself Diagnosis

Automotive enthusiasts are generally able to measure alternator output. When output is too low, most do-it-yourselfers are not able to pinpoint the specific problem because they have not had experience diagnosing problems on malfunctioning alternators.

You can devise a simulator to induce typical alternator problems with the flick of a switch while allowing the alternator to function normally at all other times. You can also place one or several simultaneous malfunctions in the alternator by means of toggle switches in an enclosed switch box.

The simulator can be installed on an operating engine or an alternator test bench. You can simulate rotor resistance, shorted diode, open diode, shorted stator, and open stator with different on and off positions of the switches. An oscilloscope to can be used to display output patterns from which you can identify the malfunctions.

The simulator can be built on a 37-amp alternator; a combination snap minibox (5 1/4 × 3 × 2 1/8 inches) is used as a switch box with a 3/8-inch-thick wood block the size of its base to fit against the alternator housing. They are attached by two 3/16-inch machine screws. Three small pin connector sockets were installed on the end of the switch box for stator-end connection to be used for diode testing. Five toggle switches are installed in the wood block. Room is allowed for wiring and terminals. Most of the electrical connections are made by fastening a wire terminal to an existing junc-

Table 1-1. Switch Positions.

This table shows the required switch positions and alternator output for each type of simulated malfunction. The output would be different if another size alternator were used as a base for a simulator.

OPERATING CONDITION	SWITCHES					ALTERNATOR OUTPUT
	1	2	3	4	5	
Normal Alternator	On	Off	On	Off	On	37 A.
Rotor Resistance	Off	Off	On	Off	On	12 A.
Shorted Diode	On	On	On	Off	On	12 A.
Open Diode	On	Off	Off	Off	On	33 A.
Shorted Stator	On	Off	On	On	On	35 A.
Open Stator	On	Off	On	Off	Off	20 A. With Noise

tion; different colored wires are used. See Fig. 1-1 and Table 1-1.

The diode connection is removed from C; two 15-inch sections of #10 wire is pushed through an opening in back of the alternator; the diode connection braid is cut and one of the braids is soldered to each wire at E and F. Another piece of wire is soldered at J to the stator winding end that is removed from C.

A terminal is connected to a 15-inch section of #10 wire, then attached to the positive diode heat sink at D which is the head side of the battery junction bolt. A terminal on a 15-inch piece of #14 wire is insulated from ground by washers so the wire will conduct

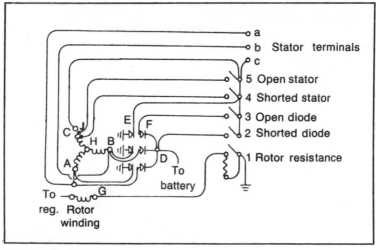

Fig. 1-1. Connections.

rotor current from the brush. Terminals on three 15-inch lengths of #16 wire are connected to diode junctions A, B, and C. The free ends of these wires are threaded through holes in the case.

Another 15-inch section of #10 wire to be used as a stator shorting wire is fed through the case opening and soldered to stator winding C at H on the coil adjacent to the stator output wire; it is attached securely to the same stator winding used to feed current into the switch box.

The wire ends are run through holes into the switch box; the insulation of the wire from C to the stator winding is stripped back to switch 5. Terminals are slid on the wire to connect one junction of each switch 2, 3, 4, and 5, and then soldered in place. A short piece of #16 wire connects the common junction in switch 5 to one of the pin connector sockets to bring the C stator winding electrical signal to the socket. The other #16 wires go from A and B to the other two-pin connector sockets. These sockets are used to check the diodes.

The #10 stator extension wire from J is inserted through the switch box opening and cut to fit the unused terminal of switch 5; a terminal is attached to the wire, and then connected to the switch.

The stator shorting wire from H is fed into the switch box. The wire is cut to fit on the unused junction of switch 4. A wire terminal is installed and attached to the junction. The same procedure is used to install the wire from the grounded diode onto the common junction of switch 4, from the insulated diode to switch 3, and the wire from D to switch 2.

The wire from the brush holder G is connected to switch 1. A 12-ohm, 25-w resistor is connected across the switch 1 junctions to provide excessive field resistance when the switch is open. This acts similarly to oil on the slip rings. The second junction of switch 1 is connected to a sheet-metal screw in the switch box base to complete the rotor circuit through ground.

The wires and switch junctions in the switch box are covered by a metal shield to protect the wiring. The shield is installed so it would not interfere with the switch box snap cover.

SOLVING PROBLEMS

The construction of a portable hydraulic jack can be an effective introduction to the fundamentals of hydraulics. The array of procedures includes layout, drilling, tapping, and the lathe operations.

It should be noted before starting that the lay out and drilling of all holes are crucial in the head assembly, and to make a mistake of any one ruins the entire block. It is suggested that the plans be studied before beginning work so that you have a good idea of the general workings of the pump before actual lay out.

Base Pump Construction

The base is made from a block of cold, rolled steel (crs) 1 × 2 1/2 × 4 inches. Cover all surfaces with layout dye. Best results will be obtained when holes are drilled and processed in order of their number. As hold 1 is in the center of the block, it should be set up in a four-jaw chuck, and drilled, reamed, and polished in the lathe.

After this operation, groove 15 may be turned while still set up. All burrs and corners should be polished from the groove to prevent damage to O-rings—the slightest burr will damage O-rings and cause leaks. A simple polishing tool can be made by using a short, wooden dowel with a saw slot in the end to hold fine emery paper. This may be held in a chuck in the tailstock and run in and out. Ample oil and high lathe speed give good results.

Holes 2 through 11 can be drilled and tapped using the drill chart (Table 1-2). Hole 12 (1/16 inch) serves to relieve pressure in the pump cylinder between the O-rings on the piston and in groove 15 which acts as a cylinder seal. Care must be taken in drilling this hole so that it is not too low in the cylinder or it will shorten the operating stoke and damage piston O-ring. Note that this hole is drilled up at an angle from the reservoir. All holes to be tapped should be lined up, clamped, and tapped in a drill press (by hand) using the method pictured. A simple line-up tool can be made by turning a point on a one-half piece of crr and holding in the drill press chuck. Holding the point in the center of the tap shank with light pressure assures a perfectly aligned tap. Turn the tap with regular tap wrench.

Groove 22 is bored by using hole 13 as a center guide and fastening in a four-jaw chuck or bolting to a faceplate. Holding the block tight to the chuck with a dead center in the tailstock, in hole

Table 1-2. Hole Sizes, Depths, and Finishes.

(For best results, drill in sequence listed)

hole no.	size drill	depth	finish
1	31/64	2 3/8	ream and polish
2	1/8	2 3/4	
3	I	1 5/16	tap 5/16-24
4	1/8	Into #3	
5	R	1 1/2	tap 3/8-24, 1″ deep
6	29/64	1/2	tap 1/2-20, 1/2 deep
7	1/8	1 1/2	angle drill 7A to connect
8	7	1/4	tap 1/4-20, 1/4 deep
9	5/16	1/2	tap 1/8-27 NPT for flex hose
10	5/16	1/2	tap 1/8-27 NPT
11	I	1/2	tap 5/16-24, 1/2 deep
12	1/16	Into #1	angle drill
13	R	1/2	tap 3/8-24, 1/2 deep
14	5/16	Through 3/8-24 nut	tap 1/8-27 NPT for plug
Groove 15	3/4 d × 1/8 deep		bore in lathe for standard 1/2 id × 3/4 od O-ring; break corners with emery
16	7	Through	tap 1/4-20 spot face (bleed screw)
17	5/16	Through	tap 1/8-27 NPT for the flex hose
18	1/8	Through	countersink thread end for ball seat
19	11/32	Through	countersink thread end to bind packing tight to shaft
20	9/64	Through	
21	1/8	Through	for roll pin
22	2 1/2 od × 1/8 wide × 1/8 deep		bore in lathe
23	1/8 × 1/8 deep		break all corners with emery
24	1/16 × 1/16 deep		break all corners

13, is a simple way to line up this type of work.

The reservoir is made from a piece of standard 2 1/2-inch od exhaust pipe, the length determined by the length of the cylinder and power piston. If a power cylinder larger than 1 inch is used, the reservoir should be made long enough so that some oil remains in the pump base and reservoir to prevent air from getting into the system. The drawbolt that holds the reservoir in place depends on reservoir length. The end cap can be turned from a slug cut from 2 1/2 inches crr shaft. Both ends of the reservoir had gaskets cut from oil-proof gasket material. Ends of the reservoir must be machined square. The filler plug (14) is an SAE 3/8 nut fitted and silvered or brazed to the top of the reservoir. This nut may be re-tapped to 1/8-27 NPT and plugged with a pipe plug or fitted with a fiber washer and close threaded SAE capscrew.

The pump handle is made from a piece of 3/4 crs as shown in Fig. 1-1. Knurling the handle on the end improves appearance and grip. The position of the slot milled in the handle for the brass piston and linkage in the end is not critical but there must be an end link to prevent the piston from binding in the cylinder. Generally, 3 1/2 to 4 inches between the piston and end link is ample leverage for a 1-inch power piston.

After the base has been completed, it is wise to completely wash the block in solvent and blow all holes out with air pressure. The other parts needed to complete the base are shown in Fig. 1-2. These parts will be used during assembly.

To Assemble

The 1/8 pipe plug that has been drilled and countersunk is screwed tight in hole 10. Into hole 11, place a small ball bearing that will seat in the countersink of the pipe plug (3/16 is a good size). On the end of the short adjusting screw, place a small coil spring. Screw the adjusting screw into hole 11 until the spring has slight tension and keeps the ball seated. Place a flat fiber washer on the adjusting screw and secure the nut to lock the screw. The same size ball bearing and spring are used on the long adjusting screw in hole 3. Only slight spring pressure is needed to keep the balls in place in their seats. Oil pressure keeps them tight and leakproof.

A third ball is placed in hole 5 and the pressure release screw is screwed in on top of it. Usually two turns of 1/16-inch graphite wicking around the stem of this screw with the packing nut drawn down prevents leakage. Should this packing nut leak, countersink

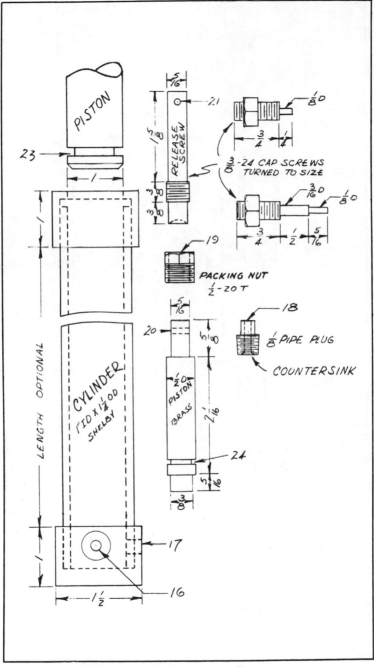

Fig. 1-2. Jack details (continued through page 9).

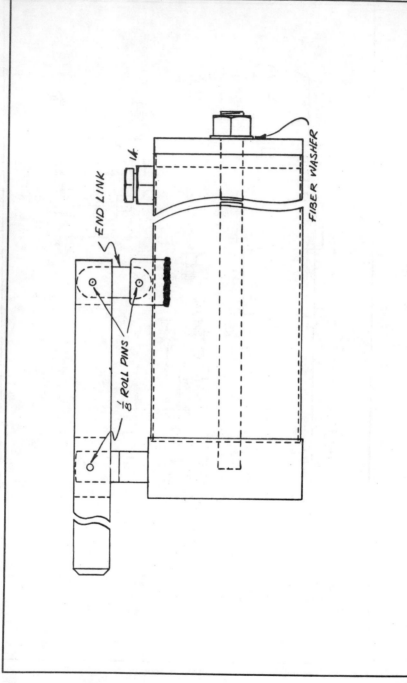

END LINK

FIBER WASHER

14

1/8 ROLL PINS

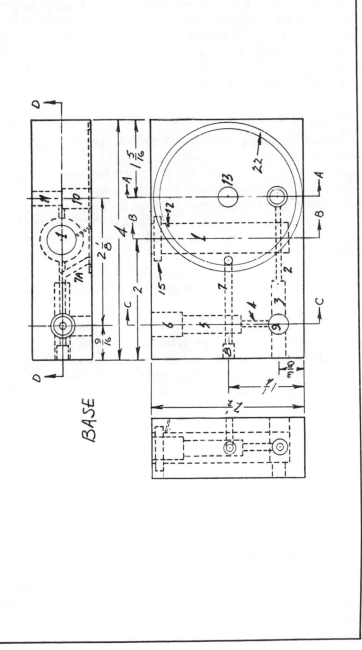

BASE

the threaded end—this will force the packing tightly around the stem. Press a 1/8-inch roll pin through the hole in top of the stem for a finger handle. Hole 8 is only an access hole and may be plugged with a small cap screw and fiber washer or an Allen set screw. The brass piston is fitted with a 1/2-inch od O-ring and groove 15 with a 1/2-inch id O-ring. Oil the piston and cylinder and, with a twisting motion, place the piston in the cylinder. Fastening the reservoir and handle can be understood by referring to Fig. 1-3.

Oil Flow to Raise Power Piston

When the pump piston is raised with the operating handle, oil from the reservoir is drawn past check ball (A) into the piston cylinder (P). Check ball (B) is held in its seat by both light spring pressure and a partial vacuum when the piston is raised. This prevents oil from being drawn back from hose. On the downward stroke of the pump piston, oil is forced past check ball (B) and into the hose and power piston. Check ball (A) now prevents oil from flowing back into the reservoir.

Oil Flow to Lower Power Piston

As there is no return spring in most hydraulic jacks, a load or hand power must be used to return the power piston to its lowest point. To release the pressure in the power cylinder, turn release screw (D) counterclockwise. The greater the rotation of this screw, the faster oil is released from the cylinder. Oil can then flow through the flexible hose past check ball (C) and directly back into the reservoir.

Power Cylinder

The power cylinder is a piece of 1-inch id × 1 1/4-inch od shelby tubing (cylinder stock is best) but regular crs will work if the inside is honed or polished with a dowel and emery cloth in a drill press or with a hand electric drill (keep well oiled). Machine both ends of cylinder square and break corners with emery. Use 1 1/2-inch crr stock for the ends. One is bored out for a base and soft soldered to one end of the cylinder. (Do not silver, as excessive heat will shrink cylinder.)

Holes 16 and 17 are then drilled. The other end is bored, as shown in Fig. 1-3, with the 1-inch hole well polished to prevent marring the piston. This end is held 1/8 inch away from the end of the cylinder with small wood blocks and is soldered in place. When

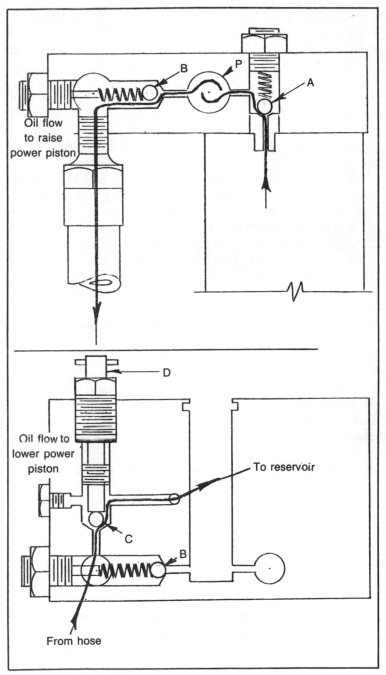

Fig. 1-3. Cylinder details.

the solder sets, remove wood shims and the groove can be lightly polished to take a 1-inch id O-ring.

Ends are best soldered with a small torch using only enough heat to make solder flow. The piston is made as shown in Fig. 1-3, length depends on individual needs. Make sure that the cylinder and piston are completely free of clips and burrs. Insert O-rings and assemble as in pump base. The hose for this unit is standard hydraulic hose (1000# cap.) with 1/8 NPT, male ends. One end of the hose fits hole 17 and the other 9. At least 3 feet of hose should be used to provide freedom with the power cylinder.

O-ring groove dimensions are crucial; they may be fitted individually, but for best results a standard O-ring chart should be used. O-rings are designed to seal by being pressed against the shaft by oil pressure. A tight fitting O-ring is usually short lived.

The operating pump piston should be made from brass to prevent any scoring of the pump cylinder wall. As some brass stock occasionally runs undersize, care should be taken to obtain full 1/2-d stock for the piston. The pressure release screw and check valve adjusting screws are easily turned to size shown from SAE cap screws. The packing nut can be made from a threaded section of a 1/2 SAE bolt. The power piston is 1-inch crr stock and, like the pump piston, is checked to make sure it is a full 1-inch d. To avoid damage to O-rings, stock with draw marks, nicks, or rust should not be used. The flexible hose used is 1000# capacity and will vary in size depending on the amount of oil required to flow through it. As this unit is slow in operation but has good lifting power, a small hose (1/4 id) is ample in size but the 1000# capacity must be maintained. Many mill supply houses stock this type hose and will cut it to length and fit ends. The 1/8 NPT male pipe fittings should be installed on hose ends. These should be installed by a machine. Do not use hose clamps. Oil for this unit should be automatic transmission oil or the equivalent. Regular motor oil is not suitable as it foams when used and does not give a solid or full list to the power piston.

Operation

With the power cylinder in the closed position and the pressure-release valve open, fill the reservoir to one-half capacity with hydraulic transmission oil, pump the handle a few times, and then close the release valve tight. Turn the power cylinder upside down (bleed screw up, hole 16) and pump the handle until all air is out of the cylinder and only oil flows. Replace bleed screw and fiber washer with the cylinder in same "up" position. The pump should now be operative. If it does not operate, check:

1. Pressure release valve—open or not seated.
2. Adjusting screws and springs—too tight or too loose.
3. Insufficient oil level.
4. O-ring on piston damaged.

Should the power piston raise but not hold under pressure, the ball seats are leaking. These can usually be seated by using a drift pin punch and giving the ball bearings a sharp blow with a hammer while they are resting on their seats. When the pump is operational, some slight leaking may occur around the two adjusting screws. As no further adjustment should be necessary, solder these screws to their locking nuts with a hot iron and acid core solder.

COIL POLARITY

Coil polarity, often a problem are for auto-shop enthusiasts (primarily because the theoretical reason and the procedure for checking it have long been shrouded in confusion and mystery) can best be met as a problem-solving experience.

In 1936, Packard discovered that a coil wound to produce a negative polarity in the secondary circuit would require a significantly lower voltage to fire the spark plug than would a positive voltage. This phenomenon actually had two distinct advantages: (1) as previously indicated, it allowed a lower firing voltage; and (2) it provided approximately 20- to 40-percent additional reserve voltage. Reserve voltage is the difference between the voltage required to fire the spark plug and the total available voltage.

The reason for this gain is that electrons will emit more readily from a hot surface than from a cool one. When this principle is used in the vacuum tube, it is termed the Edison Effect; the heating of the cathode permits the electrons to flow more freely. This same effect can be seen by heating a steel rod until it is white-hot. Watch the end of the white-hot rod and you will observe sparks jumping away from the rod. Actually, these sparks are electrons; the extreme temperature of the rod has forced into the atmosphere.

Now let us apply this theory to the spark plug found in the automobile engine. As shown in A of Fig. 1-4, the center electrode of the spark plug is insulated from the shell by the porcelain insulator; therefore, it cannot readily dissipate heat. The temperature of the center electrode will be considerably higher than the temperature of the ground electrode that has a direct path of heat dissipation.

Because the center electrode has a higher temperature than the grounded portion of the spark-plug shell, electrons will tend to flow toward the cooler grounded shell. Because of the difference in temperature, it seems both logical and efficient to take advantage of the natural flow of electrons from the hotter electrode to the ground rather than to oppose it by reversing the polarity and forcing the electrons to flow from the cooler spark plug shell to the electrode (A of Fig. 1-4).

Another factor that affects the electron flow is the type of material used for the electrode. Metals differ in the rate at which they will emit electrons; the rate of electron emission determines the amount of ionization of the gas in the spark-plug gap. The more complete the ionization, the lower the voltage that will be required

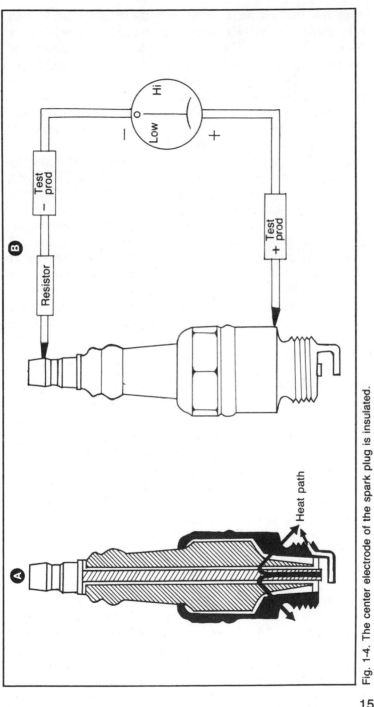

Fig. 1-4. The center electrode of the spark plug is insulated.

to arc across this gap. Again referring to the vacuum tube, we find that tungsten is one of the metals which, when heated, will readily emit electrons and, therefore, requires a lower voltage to arc the spark plug gap. Engineers have found that nickel-alloy electrodes in a spark plug will readily emit electrons while maintaining a high resistance to burning, pitting, and gap erosion.

Recalling the basic theory of electron movement, we find that electrons flow from negative to positive. Due to these two factors, the temperature and electron flow, the polarity in the secondary circuit should be negative at all times, regardless of whether the vehicle has a positively or negatively grounded battery. This allows the current to follow the path of least resistance from the electrode across the gap to ground. All automotive ignition coils are wound to provide a negative polarity at the spark plug. Therefore, the primary terminals definitely have a set polarity and must be connected according to battery ground and manufacturer's specifications. If the battery or the coil primary terminals are not connected with the correct polarity, the current in the primary winding will be reversed and, in turn, so will the induced current in the secondary circuit. It has been estimated that having a positive polarity in the secondary will require an increase of from 20 to 40 percent in the voltage needed to fire the spark plug.

Tests for Secondary Circuit Polarity

There are three rather simple methods for testing the polarity in the secondary circuit. First, with the engine running, connect the negative test prod of a voltmeter to the spark plug terminal, the positive prod to ground, the engine block. With the test prods connected in this manner, the meter should move upward toward a higher reading on the scale, indicating the polarity is correct. If, however, the needle tries to swing backward, the polarity is reversed and you should check the primary leads on the coil and the battery for proper ground; or, perhaps, it is the wrong type coil for that particular vehicle.

Caution. When using a voltmeter, be sure the meter has a high enough scale to measure secondary voltage without damaging the meter. If you don't have such a voltmeter, connect a 100,000-ohm resistor in a series with the negative test prod. This will allow you to use a voltmeter with a smaller capacity (B of Fig. 1-4).

A second method, again with the engine running, is to disconnect a spark-plug wire and hold an ordinary graphite lead pencil

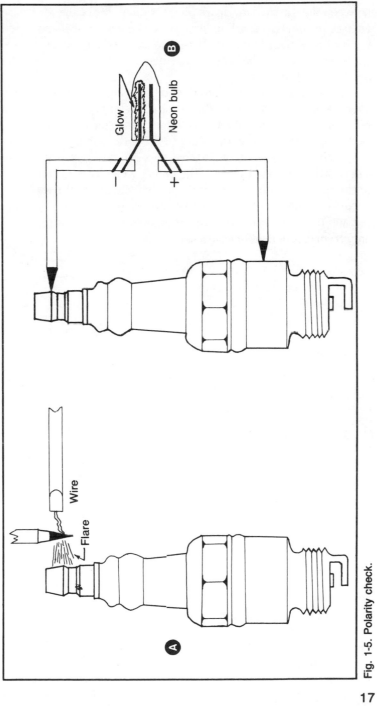

Fig. 1-5. Polarity check.

between the wire and the spark plug terminal. Move the wire close enough to allow the spark to jump from the wire to the lead pencil to the spark plug terminal. If the polarity is connect, the flare (yellow sparks), will be between the pencil and the spark plug terminal (A of Fig. 1-5).

The procedure for the third method of testing coil polarity takes advantage of the characteristics of a neon bulb. First, connect a NE-2 or similar neon bulb in parallel with the spark plug (one lead to the high tension wire, the other to ground, as in (B of Fig. 1-5).

With the engine running, observe very carefully which electrode in the neon bulb glows. The glowing electrode is connected to the negative side of the circuit, which should be the lead connected to the spark plug. If this test, you must be able to physically see and trace the leads from the neon bulb to the spark plug lead and ground.

STATIC MEASUREMENT ON THE INTERNAL COMBUSTION ENGINE

The purpose of this section is to present an experiment that will lend itself to data acquisition at a minimum of cost. The experiment can be performed on a one-cylinder engine of the 4-c type. The small gasoline engine has the advantage over others because of ease in handling, relative availability, and lack of expense. The engine need not be in operating condition, but the moving parts and cylinder head should be intact and the valve mechanism operable.

Plotting Valve Lift

Remove the spark plug and cylinder head from the engine. Attach a degree wheel to either the flywheel or drive end of the crankshaft. If a degree wheel is not available, a fairly accurate one can be constructed on heavy paper or cardboard by using a protractor.

Fix a stationary pointer on the same side as the degree indicator wheel, so it extends to the division marks. The pointer can be made of paper or wire and secured to the engine with rubber cement or by mechanical attachment. (Rubber cement can be cleaned off easily when the experiment is completed.)

Mount a dial indicator to the engine and depth gauge that has a travel exceeding the stroke of the piston. Position the dial indicator pointer to zero while the piston is in the bottom dead-center position and at the end of the power stroke. Turn the crankshaft in the direction of rotation until the piston is at top dead center between the exhaust and intake strokes. The depth gauge on the dial indicator will be compressed the length of the stroke. This procedure is necessary so that piston travel can be accurately plotted with respect to valve lift during intake stroke.

Mount a second dial indicator on the block and position the dial indicator pointer on the head of the intake valve. Make certain that zero degrees on the degree wheel and the pointer are aligned at exactly top dead center.

Rotate the flywheel in the direction of engine rotation and note the degree position of the crankshaft or flywheel when the intake valve just begins to open. Record the degrees at approximately 5-degree intervals, and inches of valve lift in thousandths, as shown on the dial indicator at each interval. If dial indicators are not available, the stroke and valve lift can be measured with a steel rule in 16ths or 32nds; keep in mind, however, that the measurements and graphs that follow will not be as accurate.

Continue to turn the crankshaft until the valve seats, and record piston travel, valve lift, and degrees of crankshaft rotation at the above intervals. Repeat this procedure for the exhaust valve.

The findings can be plotted on a linear graph showing opening, maximum lift, and closing of each valve in relation to degrees of crankshaft rotation.

From the graph (Fig. 1-6) accompanying this section, the following information is available:

- valve lift and duration
- valve overlap
- valve timing
- cam configuration
- valve train wear and clearances
- acceleration of valve rise and fall

Displacement and Compression Ratio

The next measurement involve application of formulas to determine the cylinder size, compression chamber size, and compression ratio. With the cylinder head still removed, measure bore—the cylinder diameter—and stroke (stroke is available from the above data)—the maximum travel of the piston. Displacement is derived from

$$displacement = \frac{D^2L}{4}$$

where: D^2 = diameter squared
L = length of stroke
4 = constant

Turn the crankshaft so that both valves are closed and at top dead center. Apply a thin layer of grease to the valve face and around the top of the piston. This will ensure that no water leaks into the crankcase or around the valve when displacement is measured directly. Tap the valves lightly with a mallet to ensure a tight seal. (Adequate tappet clearance will allow the valves to seat.) Replace the gasket and cylinder head and torque to specifications. With the spark plug removed, measure the volume of liquid required to fill the combustion chamber. Record this value. Empty the liquid, clean the parts, and replace the gasket, cylinder head,

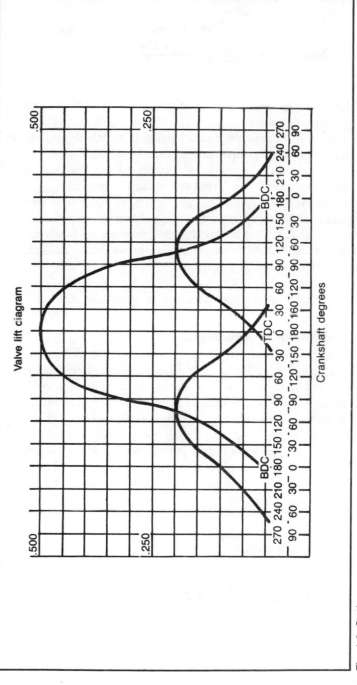

Fig. 1-6. Static measurement.

21

and spark plug. Compression ratio is now available from:

$$\text{compression ratio} = \frac{\text{displacement} + \text{combustion chamber vol.}}{\text{chamber vol.}}$$

Air-consumption measurement can be used to help understand the operation of a piston engine. The piston engine can be thought of as a pump. The efficiency of the pump is greatly dependent on the amount of air that can be taken in and expelled. To get an idea of the volume of air pumped into an engine, assume that the engine has run five minutes at 1,000 rpm (assuming 100-percent volumetric efficiency). At 1,000 rpm the engine will have 500 intake strokes per minute or 2,500 in five minutes. To obtain the cubic inches of air taken in and expelled during this time, multiply the total number of intake strokes times the swept volume of the cylinder (displacement of the cylinder). The formula:

$$\text{air vol.} = \text{engine displacement} \times \text{no. intake strokes}$$

Approximating Air Velocity

To obtain an understanding of air velocity at the caburetor inlet—again assuming 100-percent volumetric efficiency—obtain the cubic inches of air flow for one minute. Divide the volume (cubic inches) per minute by the area of the carburetor throat intake (in square inches). This calculates the linear measurement of air going into the engine per unit time. Air velocity can better be understood by reducing it to feet per minute. Divide the length of air in inches by 12. To convert feet of air per minute to feet per second, divide by 60. Feet per second can be converted to miles per hour by multiplying by the constant .68. Here are the formulas:

$$\text{air velocity (inches)} = \frac{\text{vol. (cu.in.) per min.}}{\text{throat area (sq. in.)}}$$

$$\text{air velocity} = \frac{\text{inches/min}}{12} = \text{ft. per min.}$$

$$\text{air velocity} = \frac{\text{ft. per min.}}{60} = \text{ft. per sec.}$$

air velocity = ft./sec. × .68 mph.

Today's power mechanics and auto mechanics texts have been found to be less than adequate in their treatment of measurements for static engines; there is a definite need for more clarification of running characteristics of internal combustion engines.

By following the suggestions given in this section, you should arrive at valve timing, displacement, pumping qualities, and the effects of these parameters on the engine. Discovering and recording these measurements—in the lab—will most assuredly contribute to an improved understanding of the internal combustion engine.

Chapter 2

Using Shop Tools

During the past few years, the automotive service trade has become more and more "nut and bolt" conscious. Instead of tightening bolts with random amounts of force, or until he feels a little more pressure might strip the threads or break the bolt, the average mechanic realizes that there is a lot more to tightening a bolt than simply pulling on a wrench. He now uses a torque wrench to tighten bolts to the specific torques recommended by the manufacturer of the assembly.

A simple list of the troubles that can result from failure to torque fasteners to specifications is a highly effective way to impress the importance of sound fastening practices. Here are just a few examples:

- Improperly torqued wheel bearings lead to early bearing failure.
- All the nuts and bolts that secure the various engine accessories, such as the starter, generator, fan, power steering, etc., vibrate loose and fall out if not properly tightened.
- Unevenly or improperly torqued cylinder-head bolts may result in blown gaskets, cylinder distortion causing excessive ring and piston wear, loss of oil control, sticking or leaking valves, and increased fuel consumption.
- Improperly torqued connecting rod and main bearings result in early bearing failure or complete engine destruction.
- Undertorqued fasteners at rockerarm covers, timing-case

covers, and oil pans result in oil leaks. Overtorqued fasteners at these points result in metal distortion or fastener failure that also permit oil leaks.

• Improperly torqued intake manifolds permit air leaks that upset the carburetor air-fuel mixture, seriously interfering with efficient engine operation.

The list could go on and on. But one feature is common to all these troubles: If a fastener is turned just half tight, it is likely to loosen and fall out due to engine vibration. It is essential to tighten bolts so that full advantage is taken of the fastener material strength.

Fasteners

In selecting a fastener for a particular application, an automotive engineer decides that a bolt of a certain diameter, made of a specific material by a particular process, with the necessary tensile strength and ductility, with a fine or coarse thread, tightened to a specific torque, will do the job. You can easily learn to recognize fasteners of different strength by becoming familiar with the radial line markings on bolt heads. These markings can be a clue to the correct torque.

Knowledge of the four most popular grades used in automobiles is enough for most fastener-tightening applications. The torque specification chart (Table 2-1) illustrates these types, and is intended to fill the gap when automobile manufacturers' specifications are not available. The table illustrates "no-line" (not identified), three-line, four-line, and six-line markings, and relates these markings to proper torquing. Placed on a classroom wall, it can be a valuable teaching aid.

The table makes it clear that higher-quality fasteners (specified for their increased holding power) are torqued almost three times higher than common unmarked fasteners of the same size. Unless you understand the meaning of the bolthead markings, you might not apply sufficient torque, and thereby will lose most of the benefits of the more expensive, higher-quality bolts.

Importance of Lubrication. A group of bolts that has been in service for a while may exhibit very different characteristics during tightening if no special lubrication is used. Some may be coated with carbon, some coated with oil, and others may be rusty. Remember that the result of proper torque is supposed to be exact and tension from one bolt to another is to be even. The amount of friction under the bolt head and at the threads affects the amount

1. Always use the torque values listed below when car manufacturer's specifications are not available.
2. Use of "High Stress" lubricants such as: Never-Seez, Molykote, Fel-Pro or graphite and oil is recommended when using the torque figures listed below.
3. Increase torque by 20% when engine oil or chassis grease is used as a lubricant.
4. Reduce torque by 20% if new Cadmium plated bolts are used.

Caution: Bolts threaded into aluminum may require reductions in torque of 30% or more.

Current Automotive Usage	Much Used	Much Used	Used at Times	Used at Times
Minimum Tensile Strength	64,000 psi	105,000 psi	133,000 psi	150,000 psi
Quality of Material	Indeterminate	Minimum Commercial	Minimum Commercial	Best Commercial
SAE Grade Number	1 or 2	5	6	8
Bolt Head Markings Manufacturer's marks may vary. These are all SAE Grade 5 (3-line).				
Bolt Body Size (Inches)	Torque (Foot pounds)	Torque (Foot pounds)	Torque (Foot pounds)	Torque (Foot pounds)
1/4	5	7	10	10.5
5/16	9	14	19	22
3/8	15	25	34	37
7/16	24	40	55	60
1/2	37	60	85	92
9/16	53	88	120	132
5/8	74	120	167	180
3/4	120	200	280	296
7/8	190	302	440	473
1	282	466	660	714

This table may be reprinted only by special permission of P.A. Sturtevant Co., Addison, Illinois

This torque specification table illustrates the radial line markings on bolt heads that identify the four most frequently used automotive fasteners. Familiarity with these grade markings is the key to taking full advantage of fastener strength through proper torquing.

Table 2-1. Torque Specifications.

of tension that will result from a given torque.

High-stress lubricants, such as Never-Seez, Molykote, Fel-Pro, or graphite and oil eliminate many of the variables involved in the torquing of bolts. These lubricants are formulated specifically for use with fasteners. Using the wrong lubricant for fasteners is similar to using a light engine oil as a differential lubricant.

The torque specifications table highlights certain essential considerations associated with the use of lubricants. If engine oil or chassis grease is used as a lubricant because a high-stress lubricant is not available (any lubricant is better than none at all), it is advisable to increase torque by 20 percent to compensate for the increased friction allowed by these lubricants. On the other hand, torque should be reduced by 20 percent if cadmium-plated bolts are used. Cadmium-plated bolt threads offer less resistance to tightening than standard unplated bolts, and can be overtightened unless the 20 percent correction factor is taken into account.

Bolts threaded into aluminum may also require a considerable reduction in torque. This, of course, is due to the softness of aluminum and because there may not be sufficient thread engagement or thread depth for the usual torque. Follow manufacturers' torque specifications for these applications.

How Many Torque Wrenches?

In purchasing torque wrenches for use, it is desirable to aim at two objectives: (1) availability of a sufficient size range to tighten bolts of different sizes and grades accurately; and (2) for budgetary reasons, achieving this result with the minimum number of wrenches.

As shown in Fig. 2-1 a torque wrench of one size can also do some of the jobs that a smaller model can do. For example, three wrenches—one with a 0-300-foot-pound capacity, a second with a 0-150 foot-pound capacity, and a third with a 0-600 inch-pound capacity—would be enough to tighten typical bolts ranging from 5/16 of an inch to 7/8 of an inch in size.

Because torque is defined in terms of applying a specific amount of force a certain distance away from a center point, the higher-capacity torque wrenches are longer. The extra lever length makes it easier to exert more pull to bring the bolt up to the required tightness.

But the relatively large size of these wrenches makes them impracticable for use in tight places when small bolts are tightened;

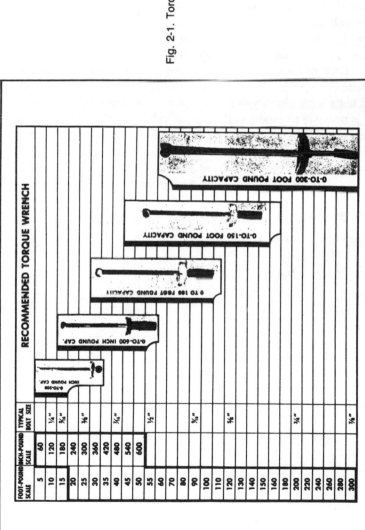

Fig. 2-1. Torque wrench capacities.

for example, in automatic transmission work, steering sector setting, etc.

There's another important reason for smaller torque wrenches. The larger sizes of torque wrenches can be read with accuracy only down to 25 percent of zero reading. For example, on a 0-150 foot-pound torque wrench, this point would be about 40 foot pounds.

Thus, on a 0-25-foot-pound torque-wrench scale, the reading area devoted to the difference between 20 and 25 foot pounds is four times as great as on the scale of a 0-100-foot-pound torque wrench. Because both of these wrenches have the same total scale width, it is much easier to get an accurate low-torque reading with the smaller-capacity torque wrench.

Because torque-wrench capacities overlap somewhat, it is possible to choose a minimum number of wrenches to tighten the types of bolts with which you usually work. By referring to Table 2-1, it is possible to establish the torque values involved. Having done so, torque wrenches that will handle these values efficiently can be selected from the torque-wrench chart in Fig. 2-1.

CARBURETOR MIXTURE SCREW TOOL

Carburetor idle mixture screws usually are located in such a position that a conventional screwdriver must contact the screw slot at an angle. Due to the fact that you are watching a tachometer, vacuum gauge, or combustion analyzer dial (rather than the screw) while making the adjustment, you often lose engagement with the screw slot on a vibrating engine.

Figure 2-2 shows a tool that works well at a greater angle and does not vibrate out of the screw slot. It can be made in a few minutes from scraps and tools ordinarily found in the auto shop.

A discarded push rod of the ball-and-socket type, a piece of 3/64-inch d steel wire 1/2 inch long, and a screwdriver handle are the materials necessary.

Here are the steps:

• Anneal the socket end of the push rod. (Heat red hot and allow to cool slowly.)

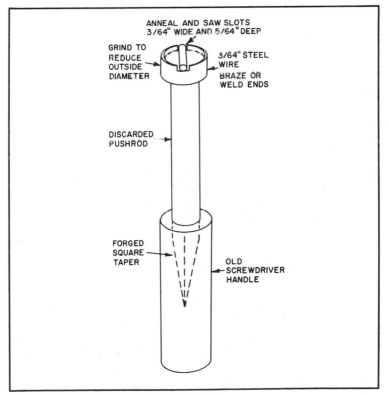

ANNEAL AND SAW SLOTS
3/64" WIDE AND 5/64" DEEP

GRIND TO
REDUCE
OUTSIDE
DIAMETER

3/64" STEEL
WIRE
BRAZE OR
WELD ENDS

DISCARDED
PUSHROD

FORGED
SQUARE
TAPER

OLD
SCREWDRIVER
HANDLE

Fig. 2-2. A carburetor mixture screw tool.

- Hacksaw a slot 3/64-inch-wide-by-5/16-inch-deep along the diameter of the socket.
- Place the 1/2-inch length of 3/64-inch steel wire in the bottom of the slot and attach the ends to the socket by silver solder, brazing, or welding. Be careful not to get any solder or weld material inside the socket.
- Reduce the wall thickness of socket to 1/16 of an inch by grinding.
- Cut off ball end of push rod to desired length. Heat and forge a square taper 1 1/2 inches long on the ball end of the push rod.
- Push tapered end into a suitable handle and the tool is ready for use.

BATTERY-CABLE PULLER

A battery-cable puller (Fig. 2-3) makes a good project for beginners in metalworking. The project also serves as a functional tool and is worth a place in any auto tool box. The construction of the puller involves many fundamentals of metalworking, e.g., layout, hack sawing, filing, drilling, bending, brazing, and threading. The procedure for the body follows:

Cut the body from 1/8-×-1 1/2-×-4 3/8-inch band iron and square off the ends. Lay out for drilled holes and bends. Drill a 1/2-inch-diameter hole 1 inch from one end. Mark off 1/4-inch distances for throat tips and scribe lines that are tangent to the drilled hole. Cut out the throat opening and file. File 30-degree bevels on throat tips. Drill a 7/16-inch hole 5/8 of an inch from the other end. Heat and bend the body at points indicated. Check the alignment of the hole over the throat opening. Braze a 3/8-inch 16 about 1 3/4 inches. Heat and bend the other end 1 1/4 inches from that end to form a handle. Smooth with emery cloth and paint.

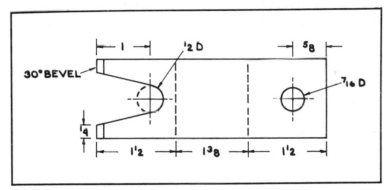

Fig. 2-3. A battery-cable puller.

AUTO TROUBLE LIGHT

This automobile trouble light/spot light involves using wood, ceramics, plastics, metals, lamp design, and construction. Once drawings of the project (Fig. 2-4) are selected and developed, the model for the lamp cone is turned on wood lathe. The only crucial dimension is the 6 1/2-inch lip diameter for the lamp. A 5 1/2-inch shell depth accommodates the switch and wire.

Making the Mold. Mix the proper amount of plastic and water, then pour it over the model to produce a female mold. Once the plastic starts the sweating stage, carefully remove the model and thoroughly dry the mold. Apply six heavy coats of paste wax to the mold. Following this, spray the mold with six coats of polyvinyl alcohol (PVA); allow to dry between each coat.

Brush a gel coat of polyester resin on the inside of the mold; fiberglass laid up to a thickness of 1/8 of an inch to 1/4 of an inch produces the shell. (A 1/4-inch thickness can cause a few minor problems.) When cured, remove the shell from the mold, brush on another coat of resin, and sand smooth. If the resin sticks to the mold, flush it with water to release it since PVA is water soluble.

While the shell is being produced, construct plywood bending jigs for forming the band iron. Using the jigs, form both portions of the band iron framework and weld together (they may also be riveted). Drill two 1/2-inch holes in the shell—one in the back to attach the shell to the frame, the other about 4-inches from the front to install the switch. Keep the switch near the back of the shell or it will interfere with the lamp bulb.

Assembly. After cleaning, paint the frame and assemble. Attach the shell to the frame using a pipe nipple and lock nuts. Insert and secure the switch in the shell. Wire the power supply cord, switch, and socket assembly according to the schematic. Attach the socket to the lamp and place in shell. Fit the other end of the power supply with a cigarette lighter adapter.

To secure the lamp in the shell, you can use sheet-metal ring cut on the circle shear.

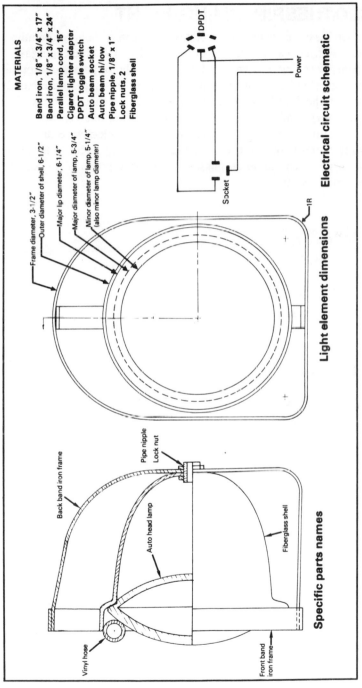

MATERIALS

Band iron, 1/8" x 3/4" x 17"
Band iron, 1/8" x 3/4" x 24"
Parallel lamp cord, 15"
Cigaret lighter adapter
DPDT toggle switch
Auto beam socket
Auto beam hi/low
Pipe nipple, 1/8" x 1"
Lock nuts, 2
Fiberglass shell

Electrical circuit schematic

DPDT

Power

Socket

Light element dimensions

Frame diameter, 3-1/2"
Outer diameter of shell, 6-1/2"
Major lip diameter, 6-1/4"
Major diameter of lamp, 5-3/4"
Minor diameter of lamp, 5-1/4" (also minor lamp diameter)

IR

Specific parts names

Back band iron frame
Pipe nipple
Lock nut
Auto head lamp
Fiberglass shell
Vinyl hose
Front band iron frame

Fig. 2-4. An auto trouble light.

35

CLOTHESPIN TIMING LIGHT

An inexpensive light for Volkswagens can be built for pennies. Study Fig. 2-5 carefully. The bulb is held by the clothespin jaws. A panel or ceiling bulb will do. Gap the distributor points and rotate the engine by hand until the distributor rotor points to the No. 1 mark on the distributor housing. Clamp one clothespin to the No. 1 (primary) terminal of the coil. Clamp the other to a ground. Turn on the ignition. Rotate the crankshaft pulley clockwise until the timing notch is opposite the crankcase jointing faces. The light should go on as the notch passes the jointing faces. If it doesn't, the timing is off.

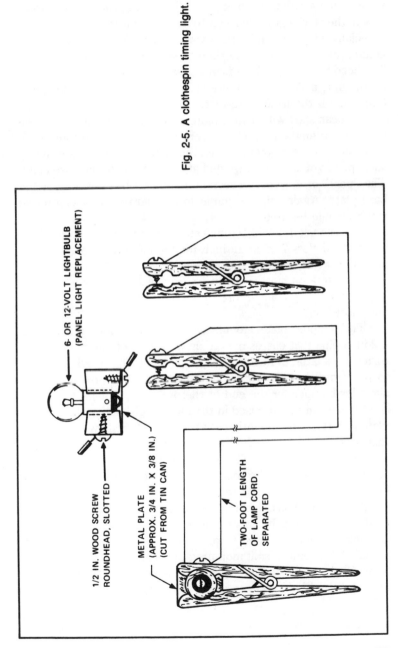

Fig. 2-5. A clothespin timing light.

6- OR 12-VOLT LIGHTBULB
(PANEL LIGHT REPLACEMENT)

1/2 IN. WOOD SCREW
ROUNDHEAD, SLOTTED

METAL PLATE
(APPROX. 3/4 IN. X 3/8 IN.)
(CUT FROM TIN CAN)

TWO-FOOT LENGTH
OF LAMP CORD,
SEPARATED

CYLINDER-HEAD HOLDER

Auto engine cylinder heads are heavy and awkward to handle while doing a valve-grinding job. When doing the job at a work bench, the work can be hard on tools and a mechanic's knuckles, especially if the mechanic is a novice. You can build a simple head-holding device in your auto shop to solve most of the problems. The head holder provides a firm and steady mount for the cylinder head, while making it far more convenient to perform the operations than if the head were resting on a bench.

You can start with a steel plate base. The base also can be either pipe or angle iron. Risers were welded to the bottom of the base place to ensure that it would rest level. The risers are simply short pieces of angle iron welded at each corner of the base plate. The "post" or upright is a section of 4-inch I-beam welded to the base plate. Again, pipe or angle iron of sufficient strength and rigidity could be used.

You can use 1/4- × -2 1/2-inch steel stock for the adaptor plate, and formed slots 7/16 of an inch for the mounting bolts. Slotted mounting holes permit a range of adjustment to fit the makes of cars you work on most frequently. Provide some method of keeping the mounting bolts secure to the plate and you will save time and "lost" bolts.

The adaptor plate mounts to the I-beam upright with a 2 1/2-inch pipe that passes over a short section of bar stock that is turned on a lathe to fit the id of the pipe. The bar stock is turned to penetrate the pipe for about 3 inches and to provide a solid shoulder bumper for the end of the pipe.

Choice can be exercised in the method of holding the adaptor plate secure to the mounting shaft. Figure 2-6 shows a "brake" that consists of a 7/16-inch NC nut welded over a 1/2-inch hole that is drilled in the pipe. A bolt can then be threaded through the nut and tightened against the shaft. A short piece of rod welded to the bolt provides a handle for easy tightening.

Another method of locking the mounted head and adaptor plate to the shaft would be to drill holes vertically and horizontally through the pipe and shaft through which a steel pin could be inserted. This would permit mounting the head in two working positions. With the welded nut "brake," the head can be revolved to any angle and held security in the most convenient position.

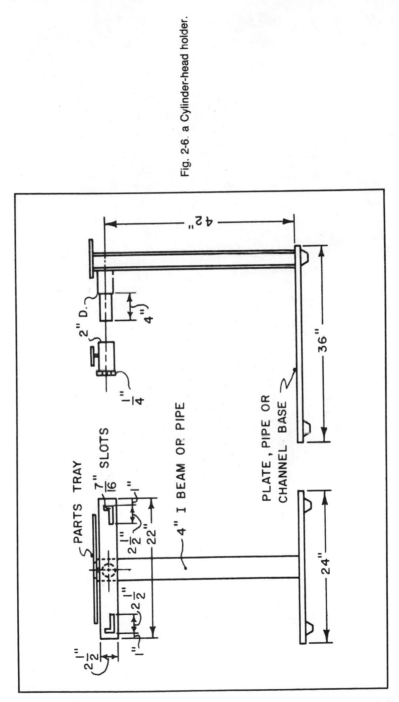

Fig. 2-6. a Cylinder-head holder.

Chapter 3

Maintenance

Lessons in lubrication, oil, and filter (L.O.F.) changes are more meaningful when related services are stressed. The L.O.F. is an opportune time to look at other systems of the vehicle that might need maintenance to keep the whole unit operating trouble-free.

Step-Savers. If the related services are performed with certain step-savers in mind, the whole job should take no more than five minutes beyond the simple L.O.F. itself (Fig. 3-1). First, gather the necessary tools and equipment. Next, unless you are thoroughly familiar with the year, make, and model of the vehicle, use the lub guide, available from all major oil companies, to help in locating the lube fittings.

While the oil is draining and grease fittings are being wiped and lubed, look over the front shock absorbers for wetness indicating leaks. Also, check the front tires for abnormal wear, nails, or other foreign objects.

When the lube job is finished, and after installing the pan plug and changing the oil filter, take an extra minute or so to check the gear oil in the differential case and transmission. Next, glance at the rear tires and shock absorbers for defects. Inspect the exhaust system and shake it a bit to see how sturdy the pipe and muffler hangers are and to find exhaust leaks or signs of deterioration. Also, note any excess wetness under the engine, radiator, transmission, or differential. Shaking the front wheels up, down, and sideways

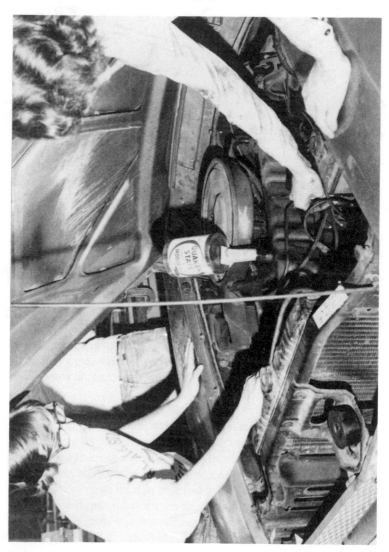

Fig. 3-1. Inspecting the engine.

sometimes turns up the need to readjust or replace wheel bearings and defective tie-rod ends or idler arms.

While the oil is draining from the can into the crankcase, perform a series of quick system checks: Examine the battery cables and terminal ends and any other visible wires for corrosion or looseness. Check the radiator for leaks, but take care not to remove the radiator cap when the engine is hot. Also, check for leaks and rubber deterioration in the radiator and heater hoses. Next, look over the fan belt for cracks, glazing, looseness, or tightness. Check the brake master cylinder and power steering fluid level, and fill the windshield washer reservoir.

When all the oil has been replenished, replace the oil filler cap and start the engine. Making sure there are no leaks from the newly installed filter and oil pan plug, check the automatic transmission oil level. Turn off the engine and attach a reminder sticker at a visible location on the pillar post of the driver's side door. Lube the door hinges and strikes with a paraffin stick.

Safety. Whenever hoisting the vehicle on the lube rack, refer to the lube guide, locating the proper lift points on the vehicle's frame, to make sure it is secure on the lift and to protect it from torsion bending, which could put the front end out of alignment, cause the windshield to break, or spring the doors. Wipe the grease fittings before lubricating, to prevent dirt being forced into the joint being lubed. Remember that faulty tires, loose steering, bad shock absorbers, or a leaking exhaust could be dangerous if left unnotices. Performing related services ensures safety.

Before the vehicle is lowered to the floor, double check to make sure that the oil pan, transmission (standard shift), and differential plugs have been re-installed after inspection. When the car is lowered, all the hooks, shackles, floor stands, and any other items used in lifting the vehicle should be cleared out of the way.

Upon opening the hood, it is important to place the oil filler cap over the hood latch and *not* on the air cleaner canister. If you forget the cap on the hood latch, the hood won't close, reminding you to replace the cap. However, if you leave it on the air cleaner and close the hood, the cap could cause a dent on the hood's surface.

Always take care when reaching under the hood. There are many sharp, jagged edges that could cause a serious cut to an unsuspecting mechanic.

On cars with cross-flow radiators, removing the radiator cap while the engine is hot can be dangerous and wastes good antifreeze. With the cooling system under pressure, the coolant comes gushing out the moment the cap is released. Many garage attendants have been burned in this way. If you suspect a need for coolant in the system, allow the engine to cool before removing the cap. Most cooling systems have expansion tanks that catch overflow from the radiator and let the coolant return to the radiator when the engine cools. Examine these tanks to make sure that they are maintained at the proper level (indicated on the tank itself). This eliminates the need of removing the radiator cap.

The Door Jamb Sticker. Not enough can be said about such a simple item. This is often the only link that a car owner has with his repair garage, the passing of time, and the miles that the vehicle has traveled without service.

Properly followed by the car owner, the sticker will ensure that he gets the periodic service that his car needs to keep running in top shape. Not only should the sticker have all of the L.O.F. information, but it should record the last tune-up, tire, batteries, and accessories (T.B.A.), transmission, and brake service last performed, repaired, or replaced. Place the sticker in a conspicuous place on the door jamb. Be sure to fill it out in pencil; rain and humidity tend to wash away pen ink.

Procedure. Lubricate, change oil and filter, and perform related services.

Tools and Equipment. Lift or floor stands and jack, two fender covers, trouble light, lube gun, wrenches, oil filter, tool, drain pan, oil, and lube guide.

Step 1. Preparation to lift vehicle.
a. Gather all tools and equipment.
b. Check for lift points of vehicle in lube guide.
c. Drive vehicle on lift, or jack and set on floor stand.

Step 2. Performing L.O.F.
a. Remove pan plug and drain oil.
b. Locate and wipe all grease fittings (in the lube guide).
c. Check front shocks for leaks, front tires for wear and foreign objects, and steering linkage for looseness.
d. Lube all grease fittings (one shot each).
e. Install pan plug.
f. Remove filter.
g. Replace filter (3/4 to 1 turn after gasket contact).
h. Check gear oil in differential and standard transmission.
i. Inspect rear tires for wear and foreign objects.
j. Check rear shocks for leaks and bushing wear.
k. Look over exhaust system for leaks and deterioration.

l. Check for any oil or water leak under vehicle.

m. Double check all drain plus to make sure they are in place.

n. Lower vehicle to floor, and clear away equipment used in lifting.

Step 3. Under hood procedures.

a. Open hood.

b. Remove oil filler cap and place on hood latch.

c. Pour in oil (see lube guide).

d. Check battery fluid level and cable condition.

e. Look over all other wiring.

f. Check radiator and hoses for leaks. (Use caution if engine is hot and cap has to be removed).

g. Inspect fan belt and water pump.

h. Check brake master cylinder fluid level.

i. Check windshield washer supply.

j. Check power steering fluid level.

k. Replace oil filler cap.

l. Start engine.

m. Examine oil filter for leaks.

n. Check automatic transmission.

o. Remove fender covers, close hood, and stop engine.

Step 4. Miscellaneous Operations.

a. Lube door hinges and strikers with paraffin wax.

b. Install reminder sticker in conspicuous place (use pencil only).

c. Make a list of defective items.

d. Clean and return all tools and equipment to proper locations.

DWELL EXPLAINED

How many do-it-yourselfers understand "dwell"? Some, no doubt, are capable of adjusting the dwell during engine tune-up. Others may also be able to define it. But many auto technicians do not understand exactly what it is they are measuring.

What is "dwell"? Here are two definitions: (1) dwell is the time in degrees of camshaft rotation that the ignition points are closed, and (2) dwell is the time in degrees of camshaft rotation that the ignition coil is saturated. The second definition can be used in both breaker-type and solid-state ignition systems, but is not a specification within the electronic system.

"Time in degrees" cannot be seen inside the distributor. Figure 3-2 shows what is happening.

An eight-cylinder engine breaker cam (1 of Fig. 3-2) would be found inside the distributor. The cam has eight lobes and the distance between adjacent lobes and the distance between adjacent lobes (A to B, for example) is $45°$ ($360° \div 8 = 45°$). In a six-cylinder engine the distance would be $60°$ ($360° \div 6 = 60°$), and in a four-cylinder engine it would be $90°$ by the same method.

A typical arrangement of breaker cam and ignition points is shown in 2 of Fig. 3-2. Before each cam lobe there is a position at which the rubbing block begins to rise (because of the cam action) and open the ignition points (Position 1 in the figure). When the rubbing block is on the top of the lobe, the points are open their maximum distance (Position A). A static measurement is taken at this point with a bladetype feeler gauge to initially set the points according to specifications. This procedure is well and good, but the dwell—or time in degrees of camshaft rotation that the points are closed—is a much more significant and accurate measurement to the total operation of the engine.

From Position A the points begin to close as the cam continues to rotate. They are fully closed at Position 2 and remain closed until the rubbing block begins to rise again at Position 3 and the points start to open. The maximum open position in this cycle is shown at B. Thus the distance between Position 2 and Position 3 is the time, or angle, in degrees that the ignition points are closed, therefore meeting the definition of dwell.

We calculated earlier that the angle between Position A and Position B on an eight-cylinder engine is $45°$. The angle formed between Position A and Position 2 should equal approximately $7.5°$. See 3 of Fig. 3-2. An equal angle is formed between Position 3 and

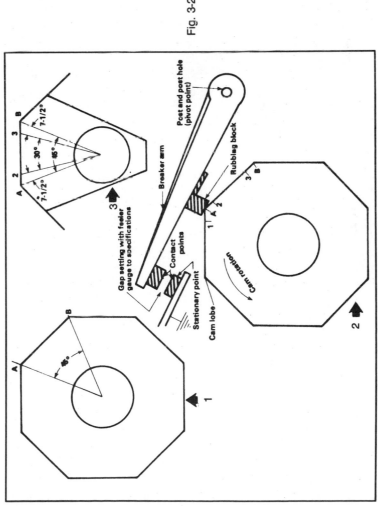

Fig. 3-2. The dwell "time in degrees."

Position B. This illustrated the time in degrees of camshaft rotation is equal for the ignition points to travel: (1) from a maximum open to a fully closed status, and (2) from a fully closed to a maximum open status. As illustrated in Fig. 3-2, the 7.5° angles formed at each cam lobe leave a remaining 30° angle for the ignition points to be closed (45° − 15° = 30°). Usually, specifications call for a dwell of 28° to 30° for an eight-cylinder engine. Similar examples apply to six- and four-cylinder engines, but Fig. 3-2 presents a clear picture of what is happening inside the distributor and why the dwell angle specification is stressed in the breaker-point ignition system.

DWELL ANGLE

One of the more abstract ideas that is difficult to explain to auto enthusiasts is the relationship between ignition point gap and distributor dwell angle.

It's quite easy to say: "The dwell angle is an angular measure of how long the ignition points are kept closed," or "The greater the ignition point gap, the smaller the dwell angle, or vice versa."

Hook in the dwell meter and note the dwell angle to see how it compares with the specifications. Increasing the gap by 0.005 of an inch and repeating the procedure results in a decrease of dwell angle. Decreasing the gap by 0.005 of an inch below specifications results in an increase of dwell angle.

For example, using a Volkswagen distributor you usually come up with:

Point gap—0.011 of an inch; Dwell Angle—58.

Point Gap—0.016 of an inch; Dwell angle—51 (mfg. spec.)

Point gap—0.021 of an inch; Dwell angle—44.

VALVE TAPPET ADJUSTMENT

Valve tappet adjustment is one of the most important phases of engine tune up. Because of this importance, it should be done carefully and accurately. Valves must be set uniformly to clearances recommended by the automobile manufacturer to ensure many miles of troublefree engine performance.

On many valve installations, the mechanic must work in awkward or close quarters, such as under the front fender. This merely emphasizes the need for doing the job right the first time. The problem, then, is to devise and master an accurate adjustment method without investing too much time and effort.

As in most things, there is more than one way to do the job. Adjusting valves with the engine hot and running is one way. Another way is called the "open-and-closed method," and it is based on the premise that when one valve is open, the other valve in that cylinder is closed and ready for adjustment.

A third method is called the "firing-order method." The principle in this method is based on the position of the pistons. When two pistons in the same plane reach top dead center, one of these pistons is on the beginning of its *power stroke* and the other is nearing the end of its *exhaust stroke*. Both intake and exhaust valves can then be adjusted when the piston is positioned near upper dead center at the beginning of the firing stroke. Valve tappets will be contacting the heel rather than the toe of the cam.

The following procedure is recommended in making the tappet adjustments:

1. Consult manufacturer's specifications for correct valve clearances and select the correct feeler gauges. (It is well to remember that the engine should be at normal operating temperature before the valves are adjusted.)

2. After removing the valve doors on an L-head engine or the rocker-arm cover on a valve-in-head engine, observe the locations of the intake and exhaust valves for each cylinder. The more common valve arrangements are:

Four-cylinder engines: EX-IN-IN-EX-EX-IN-IN-EX

Six-cylinder engines: EX-IN-IN-EX-EX-IN-IN-EX-EX-IN-IN-EX

Eight-cylinder engines: EX-IN-IN-EX-EX-IN-IN-EX-EX-IN-IN-EX-EX-IN-IN-EX

3. Assuming that the engine being serviced is a six-cylinder, crank the engine until the exhaust valve has just closed in cylinder

number six. If done correctly, the intake valve in this cylinder will begin to open.

4. Both intake and exhaust valves in cylinder number one will now be closed and are ready to be adjusted. As adjustments are being made, check clearances with feeler gauges from time to time.

5. The valve in cylinder number five will be adjusted text in accordance with the most common firing order for six-cylinder engines: 1-5-3-6-2-4.

Table 3-1. Valve Tappet Adjustment.

6-Cylinder Engine (Read down and across)	
Intake and exhaust valves to be adjusted in cylinder number	Crank engine until exhaust valve closes in cylinder number
1	6
5	2
3	4
6	1
2	5
4	3
4-Cylinder Engine (Willeys)	
1	4
3	2
4	1
?	3
4-Cylinder Engine (Ford)	
1	4
2	3
4	1
3	2
8-Cylinder Engine	
1	8
6	3
2	7
5	4
8	1
3	6
7	2
4	5

To avoid needless repetition, an adjusting chart has been formulated to simplify what appears to be a rather complicated procedure. See Table 3-1.

6. After making valve tappet adjustments for each cylinder, it is wise to recheck the work.

7. Install valve doors or covers, warm up engine, and then road test.

There are several special things that should also be considered when making valve tapped adjustments. For example, worn or cupped-out tappet screws should be resurfaced or replaced. Worn rocker arms should be resurfaced or replaced. Worn or broken cover gaskets should be renewed. Loose fan belts should be tightened and worn belts replaced. If there is excessive sludge in the valve chamber it is an indication that the oil needs changing more frequently or the oil filter cartridge should be renewed.

It is also well to remember that carburetors set too lean will expedite the burning of valves due to higher engine operating temperatures. And finally, the use of a combustion chamber lubricant retards gum and engine varnish formation and will also tend to prevent sticking valves.

WHEEL ALIGNMENT

Wheel alignment is an important segment of automotive service, and all vehicles have alignment factors designed into their steering systems to provide ease of control, minimum tire wear, stability, and safety.

The beginning mechanic often does not realize how many directions, lines, angles, and specifications—with tolerances—are involved in wheel alignment. There are distances, lengthwise and across the vehicle, plus rotational factors. Some specifications are given in inches with fractions, others in degrees with fractions. Both camber and caster specifications appear as positives and/or negatives because they read alike on either side of vertical zero. To increase the problem, some specifications recommend different settings for the left and right wheels to compensate for the drainage slope in highways.

Even experienced mechanics resort to writing their measurements and the specifications in chalk on the garage floor or some other convenient place during a wheel alignment service job.

Shallow Box. A wheel-alignment training device consists of a shallow box designed to hold 1/8-inch-thick metal alignment panels that are marked and stamped along their upper edge, and have an arrow attached which can swing, pointing to the figures. Thinner metal will stretch and warp at the marked edges.

The curved edges are marked in degrees with a chisel and stamped with number stencils. To emphasize the numbers and marks, spray them with dark paint and quickly wipe the surface, leaving the paint in the marks. Miniature clothespins can be clipped to the edges to represent manufacturer's specifications. Arrows, that should be tight enough to remain where they are placed manually, represent actual measurements.

A panel at the rear of the box (see Fig. 3-3) represents the steering axis (king pin sidewise inclination on older model cars) for both the right and left side of the vehicle. Inserted into slots at an angle on each side of the box are two pairs of panels that show the camber and caster in both positive and negative directions. The lower ends of these panels are covered with a light-gauge metal sheet on which identification labels are placed. Notice that in Fig. 3-3 the angles of tilt are realistic.

The arrows for recording caster are made with a double pointer. The longer point is intended to mark the actual measurement for

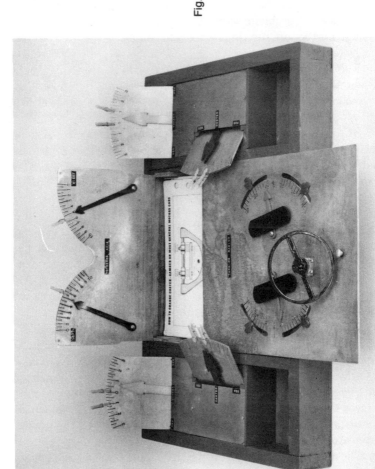

Fig. 3-3. Wheel alignment aids.

that wheel, and the shorter point—placed one-half degree to the right—represents what the caster should be for the opposite wheel. This feature on both sides assists you in adjusting the caster of the left wheel one-half degree forward of the right wheel to compensate for the road slope factor. A vehicle tends to lead toward the side of the leading upper ball joint.

Center Panel. The center panel represents a top view of wheels on turntables to show steering, toe-in, toe-out on corners, and steering gear centralization. Arrows attached to the wheels show the turning radius. Arrows, cemented to metal strips fastened onto the underside of the panel, are used to locate manufacturer's specifications. The strips are offset up through slots cut in a suitable arc. Frictional strips are fastened to the underside to prevent the arrows from moving as the wheels are "steered." Finally, a miniature steering wheel, with horizontal spokes, helps you visualize the adjustment needed to centralize the steering while maintaining toe-in.

The entire center panel can be removed, exposing a storage compartment for specification sheets and other printed material. Small compartments at each front corner provide storage for used caster-camber shims, etc.

The box measures 14 by 20 by 2 inches. The caster-camber panels are approximately 4 by 6 inches. The wheel alignment trainer can be made from scrap material. Apprentice mechanics have benefited from the trainer as they begin working with wheel and steering alignment, and experienced mechanics have indicated a desire to use such a device in their own shops.

Chapter 4

Electrical System

Have you ever been reluctant to diagnose an electrical problem because you felt you might damage more than you would correct? This feeling is quite understandable when the complexity of the automotive electrical system is faced by inexperienced do-it-yourselfers.

To remedy this situation, you can install a circuit breaker between the ground post and the ground cable of the battery. Using the circuit breaker offers circuit protection, yet provides electrical power to diagnose problems. If a circuit overload or short circuit is encountered while diagnosing a problem, the circuit breaker will open the circuit or "cycle" rather than "blowing" fusible links or damaging wiring looms.

Circuit breakers, available from local parts jobbers, come in a recycling or self-resetting type and a remote reset type. Either type can be used to offer circuit protection; however, there is a basic difference in their operation. The recycling or self-resetting, as its name implies, will recycle on and off until the short circuit or overload is corrected. This type of circuit breaker is commonly found in headlight circuits of most automobiles and is contained in the headlight switch (see Fig. 4-1).

The remote reset type circuit breaker operates essentially the same way except that it will not reset itself once it is triggered. This is because a heating coil keeps the points in the circuit breaker open until the overload is corrected (see Fig. 4-2).

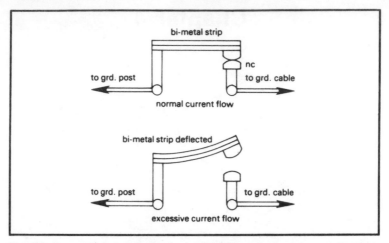

Fig. 4-1. Recycling or self-resetting circuit breakers are constructed of a heat-sensitive, bi-metal strip and a set of normally closed contracts. If current is excessive, the heat generated will cause the strip to deflect and the points will open, thus opening the circuit. When the strip cools, the contacts again close and current flows through the circuit. If the cause of the excessive current flow or short circuit is not corrected, the circuit breaker will continue to cycle on and off.

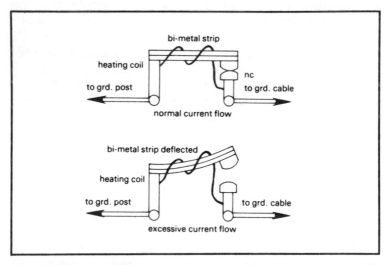

Fig. 4-2. When current flow is normal, the same voltage is impressed on both ends of the heating coil, so only a minute current flows through the coil. When the circuit is overloaded, the bi-metal strip deflects, turning off the major current flow. Current will now flow through the heating coil to keep the strip deflected until the overload is corrected or current source is disconnected. The heating coil now completes the circuit to the battery; this current is not sufficient to cause damage.

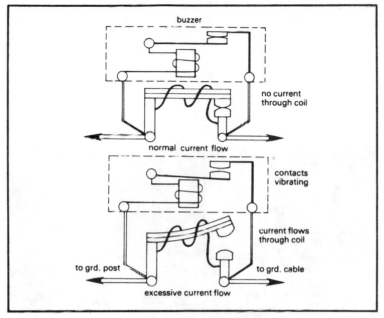

buzzer

no current
through coil

normal current flow

contacts
vibrating

current flows
through coil

to grd. post

to grd. cable

excessive current flow

Fig. 4-3. When current flow is normal, the buzzer doesn't sound because the same voltage is impressed on both buzzer terminals; there is no circuit flow. When circuit-breaker current is exceeded, the breaker contacts open; the heating coil keeps them open. The circuit is now through the buzzer coil and contacts. The sound is the buzzer contacts making and breaking the circuit between the battery ground post to the short circuit or overload.

Parts. To construct a circuit protection device, you will need a circuit breaker (preferably stud type), two short pieces of 12- or 14-gauge wire, two alligator clips, and solderless terminals for the wire ends (Table 4-1). More than one of these units should be constructed because of varying current loads. Choose a 30 or 40 A

Table 4-1. Materials.

Part No.	Description
CB-6377	Circuit breaker, 15 A
CB-6317	Circuit breaker, 20 A
CB-6378	Circuit breaker, 40 A
BZ-6562	Universal buzzer, 12 V, two terminal
	Source: Echlin Manufacturing Co., Branford, Connecticut

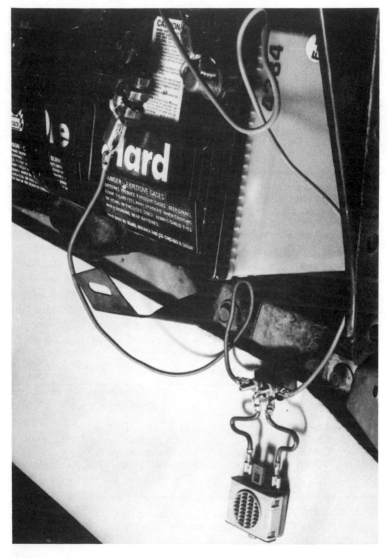

Fig. 4-4. Circuit-breaker setup.

breaker for large current-carrying circuits such as power window, power seat, and headlights, and a 10 or 20 A circuit breaker for dash instruments, directional signals, and small current-carrying accessories.

If you are having difficulty diagnosing an electrical problem and shorting out or overloading a circuit, you definitely want to be alerted, and this capability can be constructed into your circuit protection device. Simply wire a common two-terminal buzzer, in parallel with the two terminals of the circuit breaker. If the circuit is overloaded or short circuited, the buzzer is used, the buzzer will sound intermittently as the breaker cycles. If a remote reset breaker is used, the buzzer will sound continuously, because the heating coil will keep the breaker contacts open (see Fig. 4-3).

Hints. This circuit breaker unit (Fig. 4-4) should only be used on circuits that can be tested with the engine *not running*. This means that starter motor problems and alternator tests *cannot* be done using this device. Disconnecting the ground cable of the battery to install the circuit breaker after the engine has been started could cause permanent damage to the alternator or regulator because, for a brief moment, the alternator could be running on an open circuit which could cause alternator voltage to climb well above normal levels.

Additionally, the circuit breaker should only be connected to the ground cable and ground post of the battery. *Do not* connect it to the battery positive (B +) terminal and positive cable. If wired correctly, accidental movement of the circuit breaker (breaker touching the engine or body sheet metal) will not provide a dead short circuit for the battery.

HEADLIGHT REMINDER

If you are looking for an easily constructed, inexpensive electronic headlight reminder, here is a device that sounds a warning when your car is about to be left standing with the headlights on.

Circuit Operation. The problem of a possible dead battery is only present when the headlights are "on" and the engine is "off." The driver needs a device that will sense the "headlights-on, engine-off" situation and give a signal. An audio reminding signal is probably more effective than a visual signal. A visual signal might not be noticed during the daylight hours. This method uses a wire from the switch to sense when the headlights are "on." There are several electrical points that could indicate an engine "off" condition:—(1) the generator; (2) dials and gauges; and (3) ignition switch—but the ignition switch seems to be the most convenient point because it is very close to the light switch. When the lights are "on" or the engine is running, there is a 12-V signal from the generator.

The basic circuit consists of a relay, a transistor, three resistors, and a diode. The relay is wired so that when it is activated the circuit is broken and the relay contacts the oscillator, emitting a buzzing sound.

The transistor acts as a switch. When it is "on," all of the voltage is across the relay (buzzer) rather than the transistor. When the transistor is "off," all the voltage is across the transistor rather than the buzzer. Three resistors provide the correct voltage to bias the transistor "on." The diode between the ignition switch and the

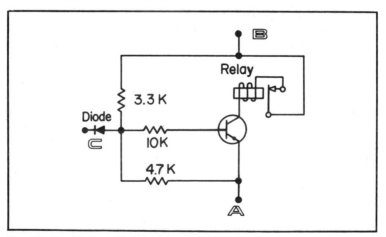

Fig. 4-5. Headlight-reminder schematic.

biasing resistors permits current to flow in only one direction.

Installation. The most convenient place to install the electronic headlight reminder is under the dash panel. Point A in Fig. 4-5 is connected to the light switch. Be sure to connect Point A to the side of the switch that is connected to the lights; otherwise, the unit will be sensing lights "on" all of the time. Point B is connected to the ground. Point C is connected to the ignition post of the ignition switch. When the lights are turned "on" and the ignition switch "off," the buzzer will operate. The correct bias being supplied by the three resistors causes the transistor to be turned on. The moment the ignition switch is turned "on," the buzzing will stop.

The transistor bias now has been changed by the addition of a voltage at Point C. This situation continues until either of the switches is turned "on." Most general-purpose transistors will work in this circuit without changing the biasing resistors. If the car has a positive ground, an NPN transistor accompanied by a reversing of the diode may be substituted for the PNP.

Chapter 5

Engines

While the method used to recondition cylinder walls during an engine-rebuilding job depends on the degree of wear, often the cylinders can be serviced by honing.

When the honing is completed, the pistons must be expanded. Some observers are quick to point out that knurling, cold stretching, and heat-expansion units are costly and that the accurate results of such operations by do-it-yourselfers are often questionable. Yet if the pistons are sent to a machine shop to be expanded, an additional expense is incurred and you miss an opportunity to gain insight into a skill vital to engine rebuilding.

The knurling described here permits the expanding of pistons in a way adaptable to a do-it-yourselfer's auto shop. The only equipment required is an easily constructed back-up tool and an engine lathe.

The back-up tool consists of a 6-inch length of 1/2-inch hex stock on which a 3/4-inch bearing (obtained from a small electric motor) is attached with a cap screw.

Step-by-Step Procedure

To knurl a piston, mount the back-up tool in a three-jaw chuck. Set up the knurling tool in the tool post and center it on the back-up tool bearing. Support the piston skirt between the back-up tool and the knurling tool. Then adjust the cross feed for the depth of knurl required to expand the piston to size.

Roll the piston back and forth by hand until you obtain a good knurl band on the skirt. Back off the cross feed and reposition the piston to make an adjacent band. Repeat until the full length of the skirt has been knurled. Perform the same operation on the opposite skirt.

Choice of Installation

The knurled piston is now ready for installation. If can be fitted to the cylinder in one of two ways: either the sharp edges of the knurling can be buffed down with a wire brush and fitted as a new piston, or the knurling can be left as is and the piston push-fitted into the cylinder.

BLOCK SUPPORT

Honing engine blocks by hand can cause problems for auto enthusiasts. You must find a way to support the engine block and keep the cylinder bores vertical. At the same time, you must keep the block close to the floor so that you do not have to hold the drill motor at an uncomfortable height.

A solution is to build an inexpensive support that would meet the needs of the auto machine shop. You can use 3/4-inch exterior plywood, glued and nailed together. On each of the top surfaces, fasten a piece of light-gauge sheet metal for protection of the wood. Stain and sealed the wood for protection. All honing can be done dry with an adjustable hone.

The engine block support is easy to use, portable, and conveniently stored away. The support can also be used for portable cylinder boring and other related processes. See Figs. 5-1 through 5-4.

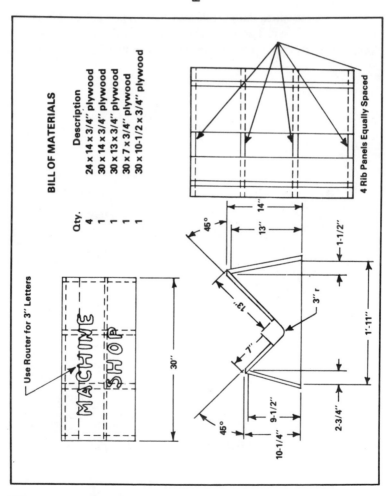

Fig. 5-1. Engine block support.

Fig. 5-2. Fasten a piece of light-gauge sheet metal to each of the top surfaces for protection of the wood.

Fig. 5-3. Quickly and inexpensively built, the support is convenient to use and store.

Fig. 5-4. The block support keeps the engine block close to the floor and the cylinders in a vertical position while you do the honing.

SMALL-ENGINE MOUNT

Tired of small engines flopping over while you're working on them? Could you do without complicated and time-consuming bolt down or clamping to the bench? You can save yourself a lot of trouble by using this mounting system. Securing an engine to a plywood box makes for easy storage and allows two-hand access to any side. Slip the assembly into the hold-down and you can securely hook up an exhaust carryoff and safely start the engine. See Fig. 5-5.

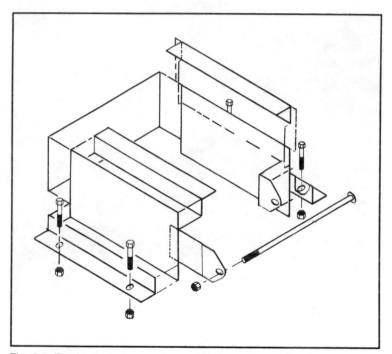

Fig. 5-5. The basic design can be modified to your specifications.

SMALL-ENGINE STORAGE

The storage boxes shown in Fig. 5-6 are not only perfect security-storage lockers, but they are also fireproof and portable.

Quick, Easy Construction

The box is made out of three pieces of metal. The ends are separate, and may be fastened or secured by spot welding, gas welding, riveting, or pop riveting. The boxes can be made with 20-gauge black iron or 18-gauge black iron. Use 5/32-inch pop rivets to secure the ends and the two handles in place. The reinforcing bend on the top of each end is gas welded where it joins the box body.

Use Adequate Shelving

When constructing shelves for these boxes, I strongly recommend the use of adjustable wood or metal shelving. Metal takes less space and is fireproof. The shelving should be deep enough so that the boxes will not hit the back of the storage rack, and long enough to hold at least three boxes per shelf. Add spacers between the boxes to prevent them from being swung around when one of them is removed.

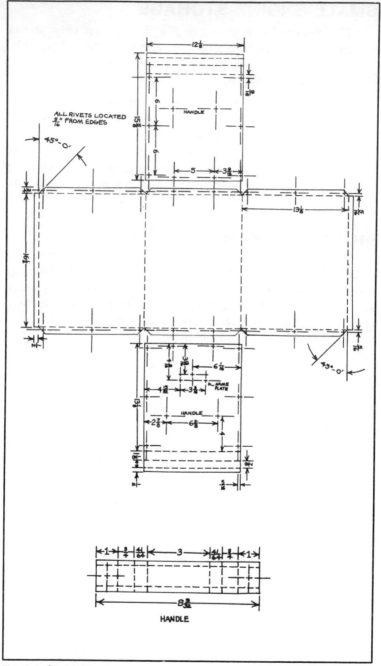

Fig. 5-6. Storage boxes.

Chapter 6

Equipment

Engine stands for your auto shop can be made from almost any shape of steel. Pipe, channel, angle, and square shapes will all make satisfactory stands. Angle iron (3/16- x 2- x -2-inch) can be cut with an oxyacetylene torch, heated, bent, and finally arc-welded.

Another type of stand (Fig. 6-1) can be made from a lightweight 2-inch square tubing. The tubing is cut on band saw and then oxyacetylene welded. It is more expensive than the angle iron, but generally makes a neater stand.

Fabricating stands of the type discussed frequently present a problem because do-it-yourselfers often lack the welding skills necessary to make a satisfactory stand. This problem can be partially solved by the use of slotted angle. In this case it is only necessary to weld the brackets that attach the engine insulators to the stands. The slotted angle can be cut by any conventional method such as with a power saw or a hacksaw, but the cutter is easier and quicker. The slotted angle may be purchased in packages of various lengths and comes complete with bolts and self-locking nuts. The angle is 14-gauge and 2 1/4 × 1 1/2 inches. Properly fabricated, this will make a satisfactory stand for light engines.

A heavier-angle, 12-gauge 3 × 1 1/2-inch iron also available. This is generally preferred because of its greater strength. The gusset plates on the stand provide additional strength at the corners. The angle may be formed into channels or tees for greater strength at points of greatest stress.

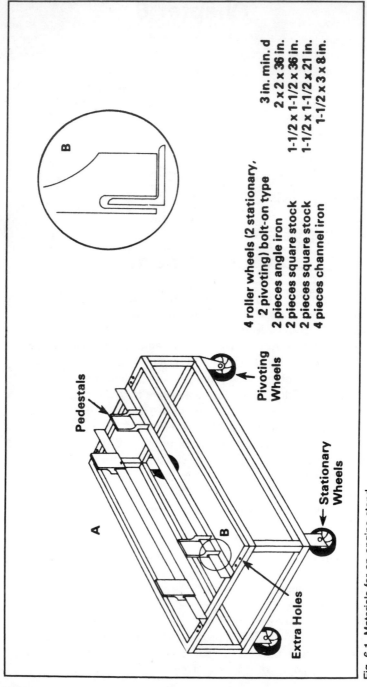

B

4 roller wheels (2 stationary, 2 pivoting) bolt-on type 3 in. min. d
2 pieces angle iron   2 x 2 x 36 in.
2 pieces square stock   1-1/2 x 1-1/2 x 36 in.
2 pieces square stock   1-1/2 x 1-1/2 x 21 in.
4 pieces channel iron   1-1/2 x 3 x 8 in.

Pedestals

Pivoting Wheels

A

B

Stationary Wheels

Extra Holes

Fig. 6-1. Materials for an engine stand.

The safety instrument panel mounted on all three stands can be purchased as a unit and will prevent accidental damage to the engine. The panel will automatically shut off the engine if the oil pressure drops below a preset level or if the temperature rises to an unsafe level. No ignition switch is required and, because of the construction of the panel, it is impossible to forget and leave the ignition on. In addition, it has a fuse in the circuit that will prevent damage that might be caused by a short in the wiring.

SIMPLE STAND

Here is a simple stand design you can use for practically any engine. Most V-8 or in-line gasoline or diesel engines fit on the stand without the need of bolting. The square-stock base has four wheels, two of which are able to pivot. Two adjustable bars ride across the top, bolted to a width determined by the engine's oil pan. For other size engines, simply move the bars to other pre-drilled holes. Four pedestals, 8 inches high, slide along the bars to fit snugly to any engine. The suggested base size for most engines is 36 inches long by 24 inches wide by 8 inches high.

ENGINE-HEAD STAND

A stand is a vital tool for any auto shop where you will be do-ing engine-head reconditioning. An engine head must be held rigid in certain positions when work is being completed on it.

Construction of a stand also is an interesting and useful proj-ect for learning taper turning on a lathe. The stand is easy to con-struct (Fig. 6-2), and it does an excellent job of holding a head in position for disassembling, cleaning, valve reseating, and reassembling.

Constructing the Stand. Use 3/4-inch hrs round stock 9 in-ches in length for the post. For the taper, use either a taper attach-ment or offset tailstock.

Make the base 1/4- x -1-inch hrs 2 inches long. Form the legs by bending right angles 1 inch in from both ends of the base. Join the post to the base by welding, or by drilling and tapping the post and bolting it to the base.

This engine-head stand will accommodate any head with 3/8-inch to 5/8-inch head bolts. One head will require two stands; thus four are needed for work on a V-8 engine.

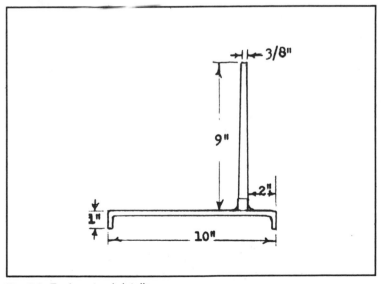

Fig. 6-2. Engine stand details.

CRANKSHAFT STAND

Overhauling the engine usually means a lot of wear around the crankshaft and its bearings—both hard-to-get-at areas, which demand accuracy in readings.

In order to take a reading with the micrometer on crankshaft journals, both the horizontal and vertical plane readings must be taken. It is sometimes easier to move the crankshaft itself than to move the position of the micrometer.

To get a true picture of shaft condition and wear, each journal must have three readings taken on each plane: front, middle, and back readings. Main bearing journals and the crank pin journals have to be within 1/1000 of an inch or a remachining operation is necessary. It is very difficult to handle both the shaft itself and the micrometer. The weight of the crankshaft and its uneven surfaces make the measuring of the surfaces both difficult and awkward.

The stand is shown in Fig. 6-3. It makes the task less difficult because both hands are left free to turn the setting on the micrometer and to turn the shafts on end when it becomes necessary.

Other Applications. Camshafts can be mounted on the stand to measure camshaft bearing surfaces. The two mounts are moveable and can be placed any distance apart because there is no assembly between the two pieces.

The mounts are made of 1/2-inch plywood stock, glued and nailed together. It makes a short, easily executed project that has practical applications in the shop.

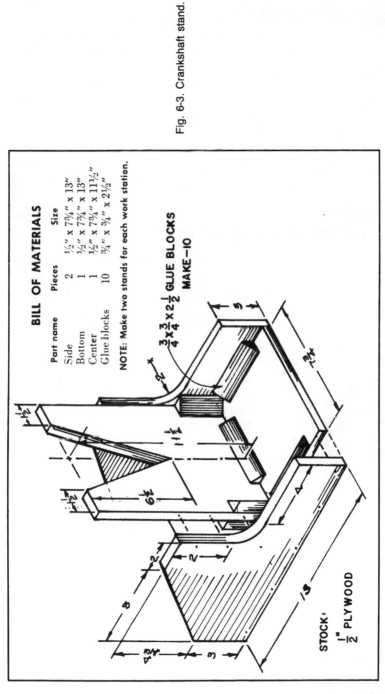

Fig. 6-3. Crankshaft stand.

BILL OF MATERIALS

Part name	Pieces	Size
Side	2	1/2" x 7¾" x 13"
Bottom	1	1/2" x 7¾" x 13"
Center	1	1/2" x 7¾" x 11½"
Glue blocks	10	¾" x ¾" x 2½"

NOTE: Make two stands for each work station.

¾ x ¾ x 2½ GLUE BLOCKS
MAKE—10

STOCK:
1/2" PLYWOOD

81

JACK STAND

Making an automotive jack stand is an easy project. It involves relatively simple skills, but requires careful work and quality welding. The stand in Fig. 6-4 shown has been designed so that the welding can be readily and carefully inspected and tested for safety.

The first step is to make the guide flange and flame cut a hole through the center large enough to admit the post guide. The guide flange is then welded to the post guide on both sides of the flange, and 2 inches from one end of the post guide. Next, the legs are cut to the correct length and angle and tacked into place (the base of the stand should form a 12-inch square). Now, the leg braces are cut and tacked into place. After checking to see if everything is as it should be, all welds are completed.

The post should have a vee cut in the top, to fit the load support, and 13/32-inch holes drilled every 2 inches (the first hole to be 4 inches from the bottom). The load support can now be welded into place, the pin and chain brazed in position, and the stand assembled. Before painting, the stand should be very carefully tested under load and inspected. The crucial load-bearing welds are those on the guide flange and should receive very close inspection. When testing is complete and the stand is judged satisfactory, a coat of paint comprises the final step.

Obviously, these stands should be constructed in pairs. If many are made, it is simple and expedient to make a jig for positioning the legs, guide flange, and post guide while welding. They should be carefully tested with overloads before being used because of the danger if one of the welds should fail.

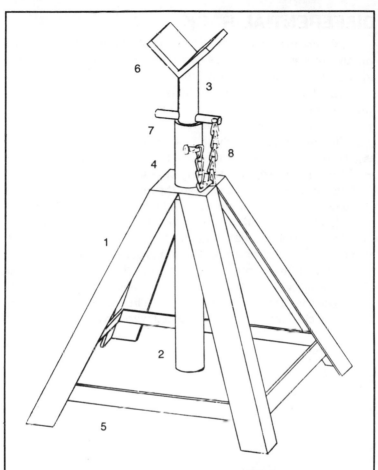

No.	NAME	NO. REQ.	DESCRIPTION
1	Legs	4	1/8 × 1 1/4 × 1 1/2 angle iron - 12 1/4 long
2	Post Guide	1	1 I.D. × 12 black iron pipe
3	Post	1	1-dia. × 12 - M.S.
4	Guide Flange	1	3/8 × 2 1/2 × 2 1/2 - M.S.
5	Leg Braces	4	3/16 × 1 × 11 - band iron
6	Load support	1	1/4 × 2 × 2 angle iron - 2 1/2 long
7	Pin	1	3/8 dia. × 3 C.R.S
8	Chain	1	6 - furnace chain

Fig. 6-4. Jack stand.

DIFFERENTIAL RACK

A differential rack such as the one shown in Fig. 6-5 allows you to store several units in a small area where formerly several square feet of space were needed.

Built from Pipe. The differential storage rack is made from pipe, including the supporting members holding the differentials in place. The loops on the top bars are used to hold the axles when the differentials are being disassembled. Storage for the axles and axle housings, after disassembly, is as important as storage of assembled units. The differential carrier assembly or parts can easily be stored in a cabinet or locker, but the axle housing and axles are too long for this type of storage. Only 4 × 6 feet of floor space is used, and you also have storage for the disassembled parts.

A pipe cutter is used to cut the sections of pipe and welding is done with an electric arc welder. In order to weld the loops on the chart rack in a straight line, use a bar through the loops and placed the uprights on the loops at their proper location. They are first tacked in place, and then welded. The pipe can be cut with a hacksaw or a cutting torch and welded with oxyacetylene if other tools are not available.

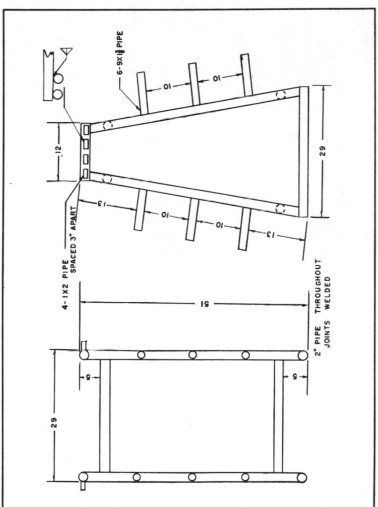

Fig. 6-5. Differential rack.

85

TWIN-POST HOIST ADAPTER

A twin-post hoist for lifting vehicles allows for the maximum amount of work space under the vehicle. Lifting larger vehicles with rigid rear-axle assemblies is an easy matter.

Many small vehicles, however, with swing-axle or independent rear-suspension systems, present some special problems. The rear-post mount of the hoist is designed for rigid axle housings, and in many cases, it cannot be adjusted to accept other types of suspension systems. Small vehicles simply cannot be raised on the hoist.

An adapter (Fig. 6-6) to rectify this situation can be made quite easily. The materials required are a piece of 5/8-inch plate roughly 6 3/4 × 6 inches, a piece of 3/4-×-2-×-23-inch flat stock, two sections of 4-×-1 3/4-×-1/4-inch channel iron 2 inches wide, and 6 3/4-×-6-×-1-inch block of hardwood.

The plate can be hacksawed or roughed to size by flame cutting. Four holes are drilled and tapped in the plate to accommodate the 7/16-inch bolts that will hold down the block of wood. When the flat stock has been cut to size, the plate is welded to it. After the pieces of channel iron are cut to size, they are welded to each end of the flat stock. The block of wood is now cut to size, drilled, and mounted on the plate.

When the adapter is placed on the rear hoist mount, the channel-iron sections fit into the mount and prevent the adapter from slipping. The plate will now support the vehicle on the differential. The wooden block protects the differential from damage. The hoist can now accept the smaller vehicles.

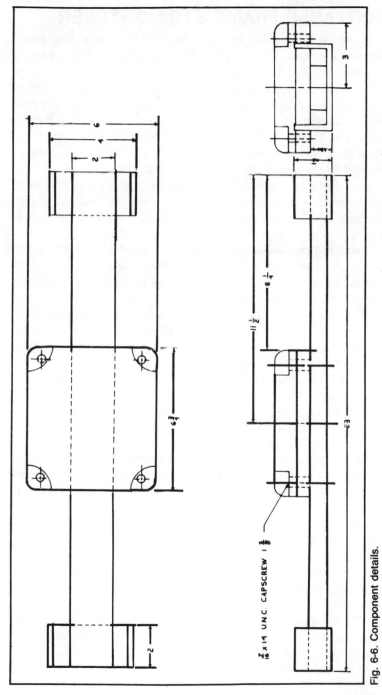

Fig. 6-6. Component details.

87

PORTABLE FRAME STRAIGHTENER

Now may be the time to add frame straightening to your collision repair program. Here's a plan for a portable unit you can build yourself.

The straightener consists of a center main bar, an upright pillar bar, and two side support legs. Each of the four elements is fabricated from 3-inch-square steel tubing of 1/4-inch wall thickness. Both ends of each of the elements are closed off with end plugs flame cut from 1/4-inch steel plate in 2 1/2-inch squares. Edges are beveled to 45-degree and corners are rounded on a grinder to prepare the plugs for welding. The tubing and the 1/2-inch chain links needed for the project are cut with a power hacksaw. All plates are flame cut. Arc welding is done with E6011 rods at the averages given.

Making the Main Bar. Degrease a length of tubing and cut a piece 79 inches long on the power hacksaw. Debur the inside and outside edges with a draw file. Prepare two of the 2 1/2-inch square end plugs as described above.

Our design called for six links of 1/2-inch chain on each side of the bar and one on each end, so cut 14 links from a length of chain, using the power hacksaw. The links are located on each side of the bar, 7 inches from each end, 13 inches apart, and are mounted in drilled holes. Mark the hole locations with chalk and then center-punch. Two holes are drilled for each link. Use the drill press and start with a 1/4-inch pilot at each center punch. Complete the drilling by using a 3/8-inch drill and then a 1/2-inch drill. Use the same procedure for drilling the end plugs.

A triangular-shaped base is fabricated from 1/4-inch steel plate to hold the power unit on the bar. Flame cut two side pieces, each 4 × 3 1/2 × 5 1/2 inches, a back plate 2 3/4 × 3 1/2 inches, and a top plate 5 × 2 1/2 inches. Bevel all edges to 45 degrees, clamp the pieces together, and weld, using an E6011 rod at 85 A. Weld both inside and outside for strength.

The power unit is mounted on the base with a cleat welded along the top edge. Flame cut the cleat 2 1/2 inches long by 1 inch wide from 1/4-inch plate. Use the same rod and heat setting as above.

To assemble, position the base unit as shown in Fig. 6-7 on the top of the bar, and weld with an E6011 rod at 90 A. Weld the chain links into both sides of the bar and into the end plugs, then weld the plugs into the ends of the bar.

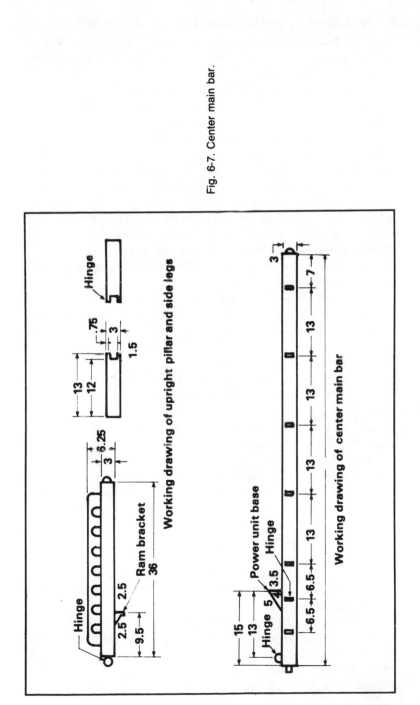

Fig. 6-7. Center main bar.

Making the Upright Pillar. From the degreased tubing, cut a 36-inch length on the power hacksaw and debur the ends. Prepare the end plugs as explained earlier. Drill one of the plugs and weld a chain link in place, then weld that plug into one end of the tubing and a plug without a chain link into the other end.

The pillar is attached to the main center bar with a hinge, fabricated from a 4-inch piece of 1-inch steel bar stock. Mount the stock in an engine lathe, face the end, and center drill with a No. 3 center drill. Drill a 1/2-inch hole through the length of the bar. Using a parting tool, cut three pieces from the stock, two of them 3/4 of an inch and the third, 1 1/2 inches.

Line up the three pieces, with the long piece in the middle, on a 1/2-inch bolt and place the assembly on the end of the pillar that does not have the chain link on it. Tack the two end pieces to the pillar, and remove the bolt and the longer center piece. Arc weld the tacked pieces to the pillar, grind the weld, and reweld for maximum strength.

To complete the hinge, replace the long center piece between the two pieces just welded, secure it with the 1/2-inch bolt, and position the pillar on the main center bar. Tack the center hinge part to the main bar, remove the bolt, and dismount the pillar. Weld the hinge part to the center bar with an E6011 rod at 90 A; grind the weld and reweld for strength as above.

Because a chain is used around the pillar during frame straightening, a safety plate is fabricated and welded to the upright pillar. Flame cut the piece from 1/4-inch plate, making it 31 inches long and 3 1/4 inches wide. Cut seven openings along one edge of the safety plate, making them 2 1/4 × 2 1/4 inches and spaced 1 3/4 inches apart. Debur the cuts with a draw file. Center the safety plate on the back side of the pillar, tack weld, and check for alignment. Weld the plate to the pillar with E6011 rod at 85 A.

The power unit attached to the center main bar is intended to move the hinged pillar. A bracket is fabricated and welded to the underside of the pillar to accept the ram of the power unit. To make the bracket, use 1/4-inch plate and flame cut two pieces 2 1/2 inches square and two triangular pieces each with two sides 1 3/4 inches and one side 3/4 of an inch.

Center one of the square pieces on the pillar 9 1/2 inches from the hinge and tack weld it. Tack weld the second square piece under the first and box the sides by tacking on the triangular pieces. Check the bracket for alignment and weld it to the pillar, using E6011 rods at 90 A. Grind the welds and reweld for strength.

Fig. 6-8. Frame straightening device installed on a vehicle.

Side Legs, Finish, and Assembly. The side legs stabilize and support the unit during frame straightening. They are hinged to the center main bar to move on a horizontal plane, and allow for quick assembly. The legs are made of 12-inch-long sections of the square tubing used for the other elements and are plugged at each end as the others are.

The hinge is made of the same material and in the same manner as before and is attached to the leg ends and the center main bar in the same way. Again, E6011 rod is used but with 100 A, and the welds are ground and rewelded for additional strength as before. Consult the working drawing to note that the hinge is positioned to attach each leg about 12 inches down the center main bar from the power unit end.

To finish the parts, degrease each in metal conditioner and then sand blast them. Spray each component with primer-surfacer and allow 24 hours for drying, a color coat of black acrylic enamel and allow it to dry for several days.

To assemble, attach the legs to the main center bar by lining up the hinge parts and joining with a Grade 8 pin. In the same way, line up the upright pillar hinge with center main bar and use a Grade 8 pin. Place the power unit on its base under the cleat, and bring on the first job! See Fig. 6-8.

A PORTABLE LIFT

The portable hydraulic lift, shown in Figs. 6-9 through 6-13, is made from easily obtainable on-the-shelf materials incorporating simplified construction techniques. It is constructed using such tools as oxyacetylene equipment, arc welder, small engine lathe, offhand grinder, drill press, and a hand grinder.

The lift, made from square tubing or pipe and steel plate, has a three-ton hydraulic jack. However, lifting capacity and physical dimensions can be easily modified by changing the part dimensions and the capacity of the jack.

Appeal

The hydraulic lift features a fully adjustable extension boom, shielded caster placement for safety, 1-inch clearance for maximum safety and stability, reinforced column, complete disassembly for storage or movement, 10-foot maximum lifting height, and adjustable cylinder positioning for maximum lift of height.

Construction

1. Cut and tack weld base assembly. Drill all holes in component parts before assembly.

2. Continuous weld base assembly and vertical column support; a low hydrogen rod is recommended.

3. Install swivel casters on base.

4. Cut legs to length; drill and cut for casters and base attachment. Install casters on base.

5. Cut and assemble hydraulic jack support.

6. Cut vertical column to length. Drill and weld jack supports to vertical column.

7. Cut overarm boom and side support plates. Continuous weld plates to boom. Drill all holes after welding process.

8. Cut extension boom and manufacture hook support on boom end. Drill for attachment to main boom.

9. Make "T" connection and attach to jack.

10. Assemble complete unit using grade five bolts and hardened pins.

11. Finish grind all welds and paint with a durable finish such as polyethylene paint.

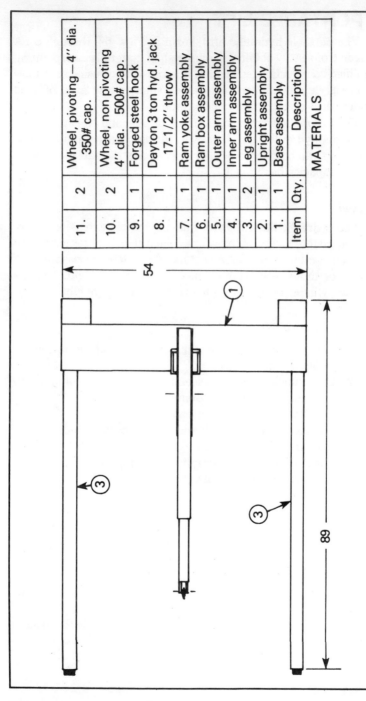

Item	Qty.	Description
11.	2	Wheel, pivoting — 4" dia. 350# cap.
10.	2	Wheel, non pivoting 4" dia. 500# cap.
9.	1	Forged steel hook
8.	1	Dayton 3 ton hyd. jack 17-1/2" throw
7.	1	Ram yoke assembly
6.	1	Ram box assembly
5.	1	Outer arm assembly
4.	1	Inner arm assembly
3.	2	Leg assembly
2.	1	Upright assembly
1.	1	Base assembly

MATERIALS

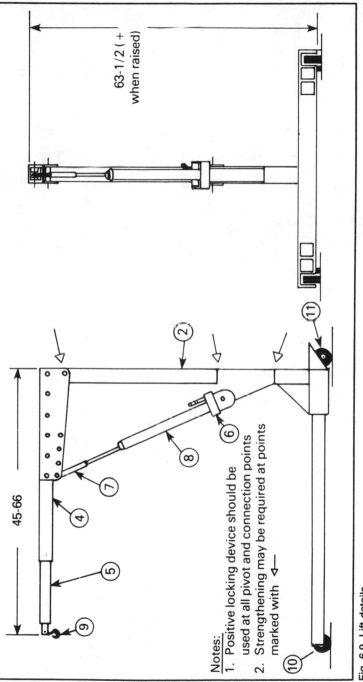

63-1/2 (+
when raised)

45-66

Notes:
1. Positive locking device should be
   used at all pivot and connection points
2. Strengthening may be required at points
   marked with ←

Fig. 6-9. Lift details.

95

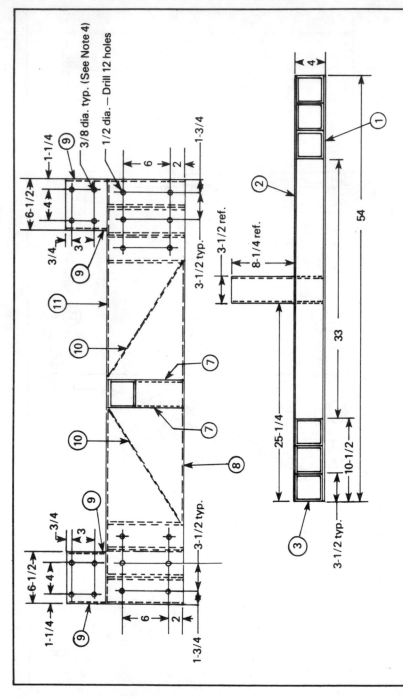

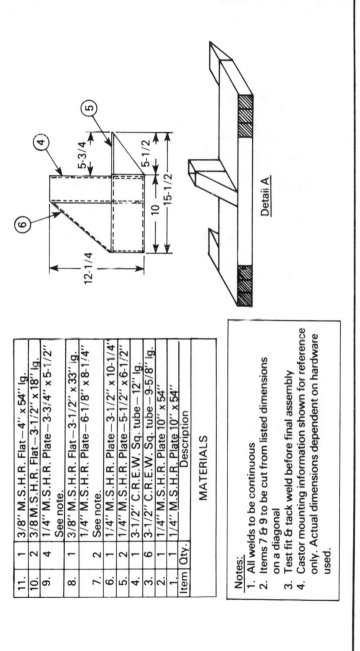

Item	Qty.	Description
11.	1	3/8" M.S.H.R. Flat — 4" x 54" lg.
10.	2	3/8 M.S.H.R. Flat — 3-1/2" x 18" lg.
9.	4	1/4" M.S.H.R. Plate — 3-3/4" x 5-1/2". See note.
8.	1	3/8" M.S.H.R. Flat — 3-1/2" x 33" lg.
7.	2	1/4" M.S.H.R. Plate — 6-1/8" x 8-1/4". See note.
6.	1	1/4" M.S.H.R. Plate — 3-1/2" x 10-1/4"
5.	2	1/4" M.S.H.R. Plate — 5-1/2" x 6-1/2"
4.	1	3-1/2" C.R.E.W. Sq. tube — 12" lg.
3.	6	3-1/2" C.R.E.W. Sq. tube — 9-5/8" lg.
2.	1	1/4" M.S.H.R. Plate 10" x 54"
1.	1	1/4" M.S.H.R. Plate 10" x 54"

MATERIALS

Notes:
1. All welds to be continuous
2. Items 7 & 9 to be cut from listed dimensions on a diagonal
3. Test fit & tack weld before final assembly
4. Castor mounting information shown for reference only. Actual dimensions dependent on hardware used.

Fig. 6-10. Lift details.

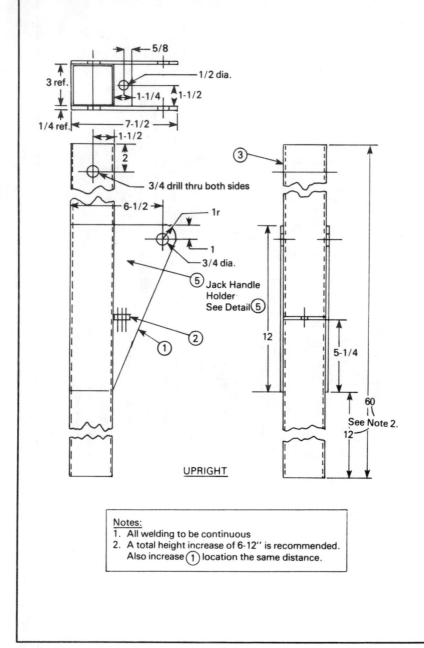

5/8

1/2 dia.

3 ref.

1-1/4 — 1-1/2

1/4 ref.

7-1/2

1-1/2

2

3/4 drill thru both sides

③

6-1/2

1r

1

3/4 dia.

⑤ Jack Handle
Holder
See Detail ⑤

②

①

12

5-1/4

60

See Note 2.

12

UPRIGHT

Notes:
1. All welding to be continuous
2. A total height increase of 6-12" is recommended.
   Also increase ① location the same distance.

Fig. 6-11. Lift details.

98

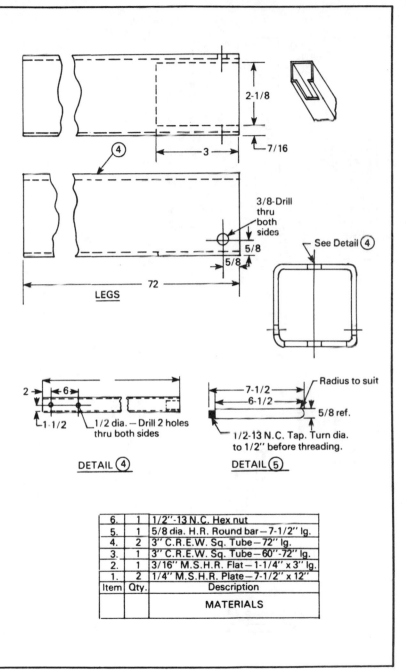

2-1/8

7/16

④

3

3/8-Drill
thru
both
sides

5/8

5/8

See Detail ④

LEGS

72

2

6

1-1/2

1/2 dia. — Drill 2 holes
thru both sides

DETAIL ④

7-1/2

6-1/2

Radius to suit

5/8 ref.

1/2-13 N.C. Tap. Turn dia.
to 1/2'' before threading.

DETAIL ⑤

6.	1	1/2''-13 N.C. Hex nut
5.	1	5/8 dia. H.R. Round bar — 7-1/2'' lg.
4.	2	3'' C.R.E.W. Sq. Tube — 72'' lg.
3.	1	3'' C.R.E.W. Sq. Tube — 60''-72'' lg.
2.	1	3/16'' M.S.H.R. Flat — 1-1/4'' x 3'' lg.
1.	2	1/4'' M.S.H.R. Plate — 7-1/2'' x 12''
Item	Qty.	Description
		MATERIALS

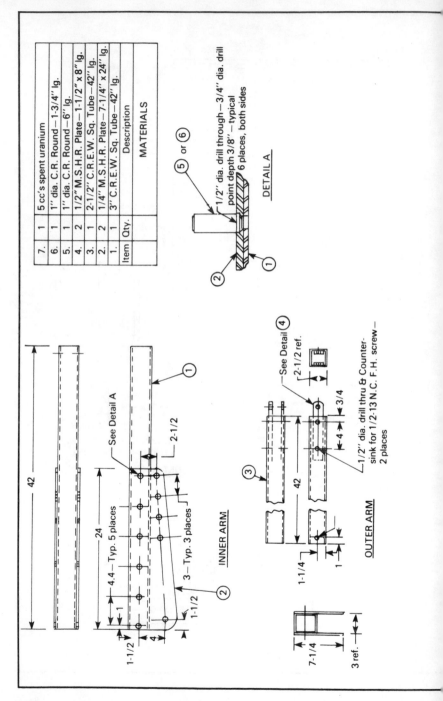

Item	Qty.	Description
7.	1	5 cc's spent uranium
6.	1	1" dia. C.R. Round — 1-3/4" lg.
5.	1	1" dia. C.R. Round — 6" lg.
4.	2	1/2" M.S.H.R. Plate — 1-1/2" x 8" lg.
3.	1	2-1/2" C.R.E.W. Sq. Tube — 42" lg.
2.	2	1/4" M.S.H.R. Plate — 7-1/4" x 24" lg.
1.	1	3" C.R.E.W. Sq. Tube — 42" lg.
		MATERIALS

1/2" dia. drill through — 3/4" dia. drill point depth 3/8" — typical 6 places, both sides

⑤ or ⑥

DETAIL A

42

See Detail A

2-1/2

24

4.4 — Typ. 5 places

3 — Typ. 3 places

1-1/2

1-1/2

4

1

INNER ARM

See Detail ④

2-1/2 ref.

3/4

4

1/2" dia. drill thru & Counter-sink for 1/2-13 N.C. F.H. screw — 2 places

42

1-1/4

1

OUTER ARM

7-1/4

3 ref.

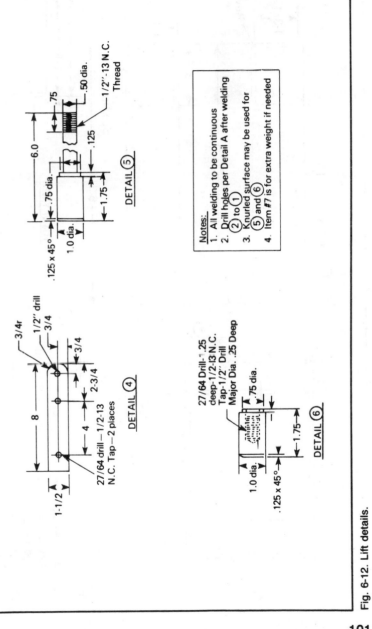

DETAIL 5

.50 dia.
1/2'' -13 N.C. Thread
.75
6.0
.125
.75 dia.
1.75
1.0 dia.
.125 x 45°

DETAIL 4

3/4r
1/2'' drill
3/4
3/4
2-3/4
8
4
1-1/2
27/64 drill — 1/2-13
N.C. Tap — 2 places

DETAIL 6

27/64 Drill- 1 .25
deep-1/2-13 N.C.
Tap-1/2'' Drill
Major Dia. .25 Deep
.75 dia.
1.75
1.0 dia.
.125 x 45°

Notes:
1. All welding to be continuous
2. Drill holes per Detail A after welding
   ② to ①
3. Knurled surface may be used for
   ⑤ and ⑥
4. Item #7 is for extra weight if needed

Fig. 6-12. Lift details.

101

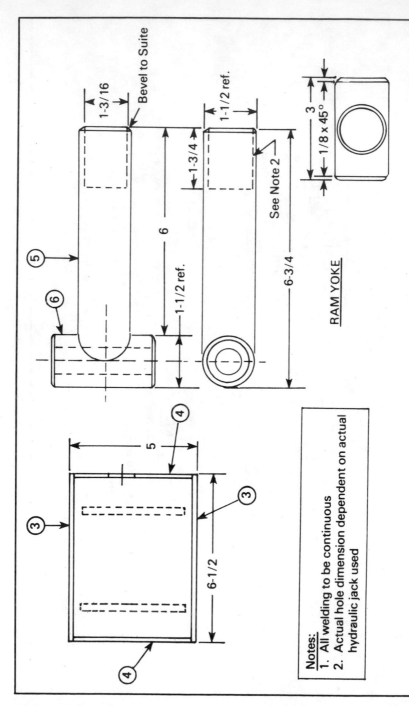

RAM YOKE

Notes:
1. All welding to be continuous
2. Actual hole dimension dependent on actual hydraulic jack used

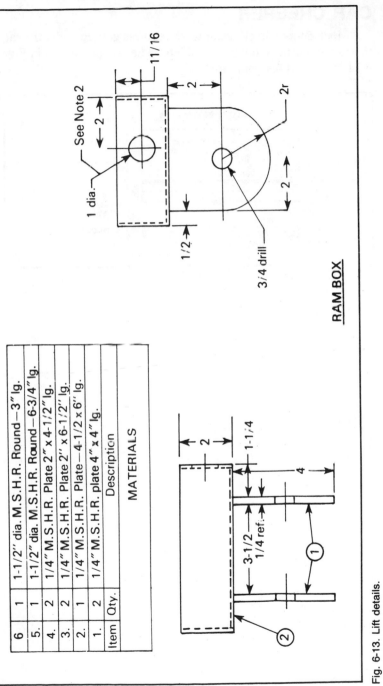

RAM BOX

		MATERIALS
6	1	1-1/2″ dia. M.S.H.R. Round—3″ lg.
5.	1	1-1/2″ dia. M.S.H.R. Round—6-3/4″ lg.
4.	2	1/4″ M.S.H.R. Plate 2″ x 4-1/2″ lg.
3.	2	1/4″ M.S.H.R. Plate 2″ x 6-1/2″ lg.
2.	1	1/4″ M.S.H.R. Plate—4-1/2 x 6″ lg.
1.	2	1/4″ M.S.H.R. plate 4″ x 4″ lg.
Item	Qty.	Description

Fig. 6-13. Lift details.

103

CAR CREEPER

Much do-it-yourself repair work requires getting under the car to change mufflers, tail pipes, oil, etc. The creeper shown in Fig. 6-14 is comfortable and strong.

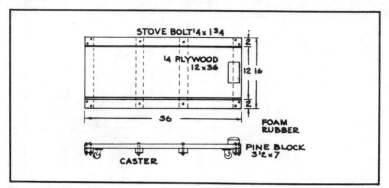

Fig. 6-14. Car creeper.

TIRE MACHINE ADAPTER

Tire repair work on foreign cars often presents problems. The rim designs are such that they cannot be mounted in many tire machines. Special adapters, if they are available, are often priced beyond budgetary reach. An adapter (Fig. 6-15) can be made quite easily.

The materials required are a piece of 3/16-inch plate roughly 10 x 10 inches and a 2 1/2-inch length of 3/4-inch round stock. The od and id can be roughed out by flame cutting and then turned to finish size on an engine lathe. The notches around the od —that provide clearance for the hubcap tabs—can be milled or cut with a hacksaw.

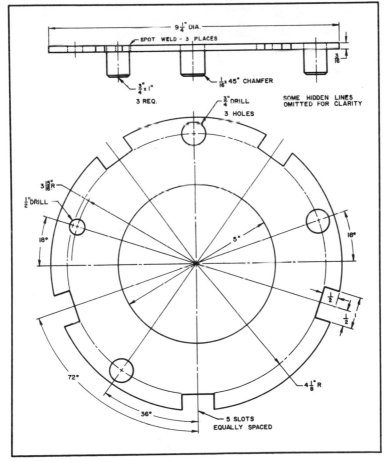

Fig. 6-15. Tire machine adapter.

Three dowel pins are turned to size, and then cut to length on an engine lathe. The dowel pins are then inserted into three, 3/4-inch holes drilled in the plate and are arc welded on the top side. The dowel pins serve to locate the adapter on the wheel by fitting into three lug bolt holes. An additional hole is drilled in the plate to accommodate the stop pin on the tire machine. The adapter is now ready for use.

PARTS CLEANING TANK

Every auto-mechanics shop needs a large parts-cleaning tank. The tank should hold a whole engine, assembled or in parts. You can use a standard 275 gallon fuel-oil tank cut in half and set on one end. Weld 3/4- x -3/4-1/16-inch angle iron around the cut edge so that it would hold its shape and be more rigid.

Fuel-oil tanks are usually made of light-gauge metal. Next build a heavy, angle-iron base that will easily support the weight. Use casters so it can be moved around, especially under the chain fall for heavy pieces.

The lid is the same angle iron as the framework but with a light sheet-metal cover. The cover is hinged and held open by a chain with a fusible link, which in case of fire would close and smother the flames. Air is used to agitate the solution. The agitator is made of three lengths of pipe running the length of the tank. It is placed on the bottom and connected to a shut-off valve and a quick change connector located above the level of the solution. See Fig. 6-16. The air pipe was welded to some angle iron so it would be up off the bottom of the tank and to protect it from being crushed by heavy parts.

Casters should be large, if possible, because the filled tank might weigh over 1,000 pounds. The solvent can be any commercial cleaner, nontoxic, available at any parts store. It should be mixed at a 7:1 to a 9:1 ratio with #1 fuel oil. It is usually water soluble—be sure to check this—so it can be washed off with water.

A maximum of 10 pounds of air pressure is needed for agitation. Too much pressure will vaporize the solvent; and, of course, this is a fire hazard.

The real heavy deposits will have to be scraped off, but if you let auto parts with heavy deposits soak for a half hour and turn the air on for an hour or less you will be amazed at the results.

In either shape, a small shelf for scraping parts, preferably over the air connections, is handy. An old wheel rim attached to the side also is convenient storage for the air hose. When figuring the cost of the cleaner, length × width × height of the cleaner in inches divided by 231 will give you the number of total gallons necessary for one fill. On the average, one and one-half tankfuls should take care of you for the year, depending, naturally, on the amount of parts you clean.

For a small-parts tank, an old wringer-type washing machine, with the machinery removed, works very well. A medical sterilizer

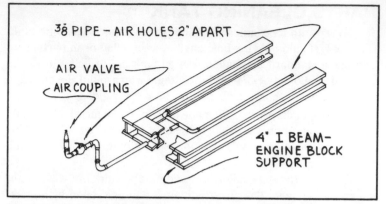

Fig. 6-16. Cleaning tank agitator.

such as from federal surplus has a hydraulic tray in it. The steam pipes in the bottom are ideal for compressed air. It is of stainless steel so that it is easy to keep clean.

These tanks are not as elaborate as the commercial ones, but this is one piece of equipment you can make yourself. So if a parts tank is needed, look around—you probably have the making in your own shop.

Chapter 7

Shop Work

Dents or creases in auto bodies are not always in accessible locations for making repairs with standard techniques and tools. This slide hammer, a useful, functional, specialized auto tool, will remove dents from the outside. The hammer is an easily constructed shop-made tool.

The slide hammer can be constructed by various methods. You can use an engine lathe to form a heavy-duty tool or a lighter hammer can be made using standard bench working techniques.

Figure 7-1 shows a bench-made hammer. A vise, file, hammer, drill press, and taps and dies are the common tools needed for construction. A more complex approach to hammer construction uses the engine lathe. Figure 7-2 is a general outline for developing the project. The engine lathe method produces a tool with a professional flair.

Lathe Method Construction
Slide—18″ of 1″ dia crs
1. Cut stock to size.
2. Face off both ends.
3. Center drill one end.
4. Secure in lathe; turn to required diameter (.500″) and required length.
5. Remove fillet.

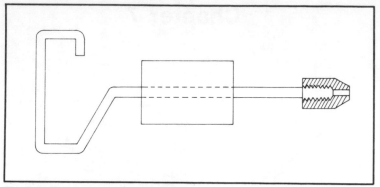

Fig. 7-1. Slide hammer, bench method.

6. Thread 1/2-13 to required length.

7. Knurl required length.

Weight—5″ of 2″ dia crs

1. Cut stock to size.

2. Face off both ends.

3. Center punch hole and drill a .562″ hole through weight.

4. Knurl. It may be necessary to knurl one section at a time. Reverse the weight and match knurl. Remember to protect the knurled section from the chuck.

Cap—1.5″ of 1″ dia crs

1. Cut stock to size.

2. Face off both ends and center punch.

3. Drill required holes to depth.

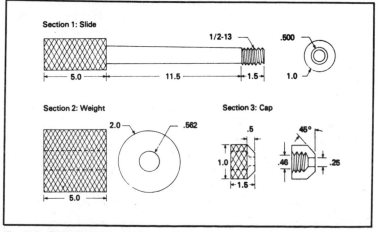

Fig. 7-2. Slide hammer, lathe method.

4. Thread internally to 1/2-13.
5. Knurl to required length.
6. Form taper by compound rest method.

Using the Hammer. Position a self-tapping sheet metal screw between the cap and the slide section of the hammer. Drill an undersized hole into the deepest portion of the dent. Fit the assembled hammer in this hole. Hammer weight is forced outward, thus pulling the dent from the outside. Use a pick hammer to form the edges of the dent. If the dent is large, apply the hammer at several different locations.

The screw hole can be filled with putty and covered with fiberglass, which will form the final contour of the dent and fill out tool holes.

REMOVING BROKEN BOLTS

Broken bolt removal is one project where shop safety is a must: always wear safety glasses, always wear leather shoes, and always use the correct tool for the job. See Table 7-1.

Procedure

1. Locate and center punch solid metal block for three holes to be drilled and threaded (Fig. 7-3).

2. Drill all marks with 1/8-inch drill bit 3/4 of an inch deep using progressive drill method.

3. Drill two holes to proper size for 3/8 of an inch -16 tap.

4. Using starting, plug, and bottoming taps make threads to bottom of hole.

5. Install 3/8 of an inch -16 bolt approximately 2 1/2-inch long into threaded hole and bottom it.

6. Cut off bolt approximately 1 inch above top of block using hacksaw.

Table 7-1. Materials, Tools, and Equipment.

Material needed

Solid metal block approximately 1-1/2″ × 2-1/2″ × 2-1/2″
3/8″-16 bolt approximately 2-1/2″ long

Tools and equipment needed

Drill press
Tap drill chart
6″ scale
Hacksaw
2 fine-toothed hacksaw blades
Fractional drill bit set 1/16″-1/2″
Taps 3/8″-16 starting, plug, bottoming
Various types of screw extractors and E-Z outs
1/4″ or 3/8″ portable electric hand drill
Drill vise
Hand oiler
File
Center punch
Ball-peen hammer
14″ pipe wrench
Vise grip pliers
Adjustable wrench
Screwdriver

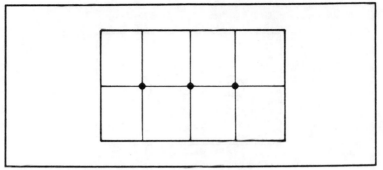

Fig. 7-3. Hole locations.

7. File top of cut off bolt flat.

8. Put two blades in the hacksaw and cut a screwdriver slot in bolt (Fig. 7-4).

9. File two flats on sides of bolt. Demonstrate use of screwdriver, adjustable wrench, vise grips, and pipe wrench to remove broken bolt.

10. Cut bolt flush with top of block. Demonstrate use of center punch and ball-peen hammer to remove bolt.

11. Locate and center punch exact center of broken bolt (Fig. 7-5).

12. Drill hole using 1/8-inch drill bit approximately 1/2 inch deep.

13. Use progressive drill method to drill to proper size for screw extractor and remove broken portion of bolt.

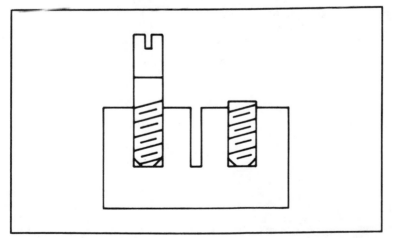

Fig. 7-4. Cut a slot in the bolt.

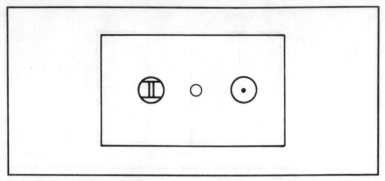

Fig. 7-5. Punch the center of the bolt.

    14. Inspect threads for damage—clean up with tap. Recheck for fitness of threads to be used again.

    15. Drill one hole to accept 1/8-inch pipe thread.

    16. Use 1/8 -27 tap to thread hole.

HYDRAULIC PRESS

Auto mechanics frequently need a hydraulic press for installing and removing wrist pins, bearings, seals, gears, etc. You can easily build a press from used or scrap materials. The project will involve arc welding and drilling. See Table 7-2.

Use 1/2-inch bolts to assemble the main frame, and 4 3/8-inch bolts and tubing spacers to hold the table together. The two assemblies provide guides for the sliding ram and return springs. Welding is required in two places. The first weld holds the 1-inch section of pipe to the 7 1/8-inch piece of channel to act as the jack stop. The second weld attaches the 4-inch ram to the flat iron guide bar. Drill holes at 6-inch intervals along the uprights of the press to accommodate varying lengths of auto parts. The table is held at the desired height during pressing by 1/2-inch bolts.

Table 7-2. Materials.

Qty.	Description
1	5 ton hydraulic jack
2	4″ channel iron × 6′
6	4″ channel iron × 29″
1	4″ channel iron × 7-1/8″
2	2″ × 2″ angle iron × 29″
1	1/2″ × 3″ × 28-1/2″ flat iron for guide bar
1	1-1/2″ × 4″ round bar stock for ram
2	8″ tension type springs Steel pipe fittings
2	1/2″ × 12″ pipe, threaded both ends
4	1/2″ base flanges
4	1/2″ × 2-1/2″ nipples
4	1/2″ elbows
4	3/8″ × 4-3/8″ tubing for table spacer
1	1-1/2″ dia × 1″ pipe
10	1/2″ × 5″ machine bolts with nuts and washers
6	3/8″ × 5″ machine bolts with nuts and washers
16	3/8″ × 2″ flat head machine bolts, nuts, and washers

SHOP MATH

The function $Y = f$ (angle θ) has little meaning to the auto enthusiast and may help reinforce a negative attitude about mathematics and graphing. But if it is applied to a practical problem in the auto shop, it takes on a real meaning.

A single-cylinder gasoline engine with the head removed and a degree wheel attached to the crankshaft is an excellent trainer to show that the function $Y = f$ (angle θ) and its graph represent something practical. Beginning with the piston at top dead center (TDC) rotate the crankshaft through 30-degree increments and measure travel of the piston down the cylinder wall with a steel rule. Using a completed data sheet (Fig. 7-6), you can plot a graph (Fig. 7-7).

Figure 7-7 is a graph of the function $Y = f$ (angle θ), not derived through table or calculator values, but through measured angles and distances. By plotting it, you will see the relevance of graphs and mathematical function. Further analysis of piston velocity and acceleration may be completed using the same data.

Rotation (degrees)	Piston travel (inches)
0 (TDC)	0.00
30	0.15
60	0.53
90	1.00
120	1.40
150	1.66
180 (BDC)	1.75
210	1.66
240	1.40
270	1.00
300	0.53
330	0.15
360 (TDC)	0.00

TDC = Top Dead Center
BDC = Bottom Dead Center

Fig. 7-6. Data sheet.

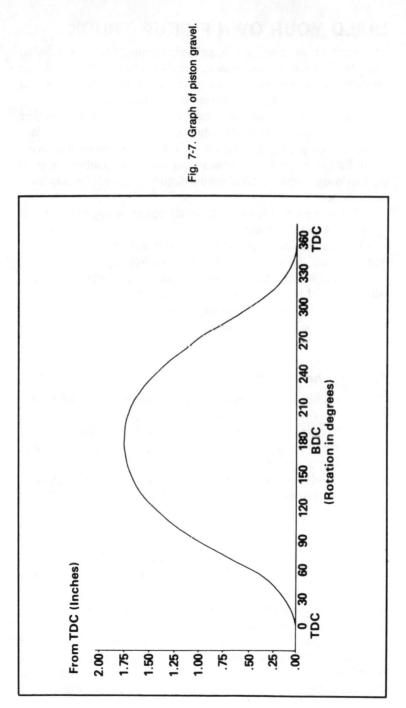

Fig. 7-7. Graph of piston gravel.

BUILD YOUR OWN PICKUP TRUCK

Practical, exciting, and imaginative projects are not easy to come by. The conversion of an automobile into a pickup truck can prove to be an excellent class project and an opportunity for you to use your imagination in solving a variety of problems.

The project will allow you the opportunity to examine a number of mechanisms and automotive design features such as door glass controls, door and trunk locks, door glass track adjustment devices, trunk lid hinge and counter balancing systems, headliner retaining hardware, some electrical wiring circuits, and general auto body construction.

This project will not only be challenging to build, but it will be useful when completed.

The conversion project will provide experience in a variety of metal cutting, fastening, and forming techniques.

The project is intentionally designed to use only simple and readily available tools. The tools you will need are limited to a 1/4-inch electric drill, a two-speed electric sabre saw, a hand hacksaw, a ball-peen hammer, a pair of pliers, and assorted wrenches and screwdrivers.

Planning the Project

Flame cutting and welding equipment were ruled out for three reasons: possible fire hazard from upholstery and gasoline; warping and buckling of the metal and heat damage to the paint; and because welding thin auto body metal requires a degree of skill beyond that of the students.

Hand tools and the two-speed sabre saw were used for all cuts. Some of the braces and brackets were cut with a cold chisel. Rivets, sheet-metal screws, machine screws, and pop rivets were used for fastenings.

The legality and licensing of the conversion called for some paperwork. In California, a passenger car may be converted and then licensed as a pickup truck by merely having the completed truck weighed; completing the proper forms, and paying a nominal transfer fee. Check with your state vehicle departments for regulations relating to the modification of motor vehicles.

Much of the material from the car itself could be utilized. For example, the rear glass section was cut out and moved up to just behind the front door post. The section cut from the top became the back of the cab. The trunk lid was cut to form the tailgate, and the remaining trunk lid metal provided sufficient material to finish off the pickup bed.

Materials

The only material purchased was one sheet of 5/8-in. marine plywood used for the floor of the pickup bed, one sheet of 3/8-in. marine plywood for the side walls of the bed, a pair of eight-foot 2×4's which were used for the cribbing under the floor of the bed, and one length of electrical conduit used to form the handrails.

A photo enlargement of the automobile was cut and pasted so students could visualize the final appearance of the truck and to help determine location of the cuts to be made on the car.

Preparing the Car

Remove the rear seat and back rest, remove the rear floor mat, remove the dome light, and to carefully disconnect the rear portion of the headliner. The headliner is rolled up and tucked under one of the headliner hoops just ahead of the front door post to keep it out of the way when driving and while working on the conversion.

Remove the glass cranks, door panels, glass, and glass control mechanisms. The rear door locks were not removed, and the outside rear door handles were left in place to serve as tie-down cleats. Remove the trunk lid. Extra care must be exercised when removing the trunk lid and hinges. The counter balance springs are heavily loaded and can fly out with sudden and *extreme* force when disconnected.

All parts and materials should be saved for possible use in completing the truck. For instance, the rear floor mat and the rear door panels can be cut down to help finish the interior of the cab. The headliner is cut, trimmed, and tucked into place to finish around the dome light and rear glass. The remaining headliner material is cemented to the upper rear sides of the cab. The door trim beading is used to hold some of the headliner material in place and to cover exposed edges of sheet metal at the lower part of the rear glass.

Cutting and Fitting

After the preparatory work is completed, plan the cutting sequences. The rear door glass frames are cut at the lower sill line with a hand hacksaw. Make a careful study of the front and rear cuts across the top. Make pencil marks and place strips of masking tape on each side of the pencil lines. The masking tape protects the paint from scratches during the cutting operation with the sabre saw. The slow cutting speed is used during this operation. By working carefully and avoiding scratches, the truck will not have to be repainted after it was completed. A small jar of touch-up paint is all that is needed to cover all rivets, screws, and exposed edges of sheet metal.

After the rear glass section and the top section are removed, a cut is made on each side from the rear of the trunk to the rear doors. This is done to provide a flat surface at the top rear of the bed and to give the truck a wider bed. All burrs and sharp edges are removed with a 10-inch mill file. The rear glass section is then placed forward in position to start forming the cab. A 1 1/2-inch lap joint is allowed, and the section is temporarily fastened in place with sheet metal screws. Small V-shaped segments are cut out of the metal of the rear glass section to make it conform to the curvature of the top.

A piece of cardboard is used to make a pattern for the back of the cab. The pattern is transferred to the section that had been cut from the car top and the metal is cut to shape with tin snips. About 1 1/2 inches of material is allowed for bending inward to form the bottom flange. Snip cuts are required to form the metal around the driveshaft tunnel and to conform to the foot wells of the car floor. Sheet-metal screws are used to secure the assembly.

Care must be taken to avoid hitting gasoline, and hydraulic tubing and electrical wires when drilling for the sheet-metal screws. Also avoid installing screws into the driveshaft tunnel because they may cut into the driveshaft.

After the cab sections are properly fitted, the unit is dismantled and windshield-sealing compound is spread on all joints. The body sections are replaced and refastened with the screws. Then the screws are removed one at a time and each hole is drilled out to rivet size. The hole is slightly countersunk on the outside of the cab. A tinners rivet is then inserted and bucked from the inside and peened tight from the outside of the cab. To get a weathertight seal, the rivets are spaced about 1 inch apart. Pop rivets are used to fasten the rear cab section to the floor and around the driveshaft tunnel. Excess windshield compound is cleaned off by using a bit of paint thinner and wiping with a rag. (Caution: Do not use lacquer thinner.)

A generous coating of Hydraseal is spread on the floor joint to waterseal that section. Windshield sealing compound is used to caulk all other small openings that remain. Several holes can be punched into the floor on the outside of the cab so that water will not collect in these wells.

Constructing the Bed

The 2 × 4s are fabricated to form the cribbing to support the plywood floor of the bed. The cribbing is lag screwed in place from beneath the truck. A cardboard pattern is made of the floor and the shape is traced on the plywood. The piece is cut with the sabre saw, fitted with a wood-cutting blade, and set for high speed.

The side walls of the bed are cut from 3/8-inch plywood and fastened to the truck body. Sheet-metal angles made from the trunk lid material are used to attach the top of the bed sides and the joint where the side walls and the bed floor meet. The inside of the bed is finished with two coats of porch and deck enamel.

Load capacity of the example truck is about 800 pounds. The capacity can be increased by the installation of over-load springs or spring-assisted heavy duty shock absorbers.

The finished truck has many positive features, including easy handling and excellent visibility; easily available and inexpensive repair parts; space behind the seat for the spare tire, a tool box, and two agile passengers. Approximately 60 man-hours are required to complete the project.

PICKUP TRUCK BOX COVER

The pickup truck has come into its own. The homeowner of today, busy collecting power mowers, home workshop tools and materials, camping equipment, and Cub Scouts, finds the pickup truck indispensable for his needs.

Your pickup truck can be fitted with a box cover that can be locked when carrying tools, materials, camping equipment, or luggage. Furthermore, the cover doubles as a shelter for sleeping when inclement weather strikes the camping site. Another advantage is its year-round protection of the truck bed from weathering.

This project involves a number of learning processes in its construction and finishing, such as design and planning, machine operations, assembling, metal fabrication, etc.

Making the Frame. All parts of the basic frame are 3/4 of an inch thick. See Table 7-3 and Fig. 7-8 for dimensions (dimensions must be adjusted to fit individual trucks). Assemble rails and frames A, B, C, and D with eight 1 1/2-inch wood screws (be sure to use brass or cadmium plated screws) and a plastic resin glue. Plane a bevel on center rail and the two side skirts.

Next, cut two 1/4- × -29 1/4- × -80 inch exterior A.C. Douglas fir plywood pieces and fasten them to assembled frame with glue and #5 1/2-inch fh wood screws approximately every 6 inches. Plane off any excess overhang on plywood. At this point it is advisable to sand all exposed parts of the frame.

Cut all metal angle trim to length and cut 45-degree angles on

Table 7-3. Materials.

Amount	Size	Name
2	3/4 × 2 3/4 × 80	side rail
1	3/4 × 2 × 80	top rail
1	3/4 × 6 × 57 1/2	A
1	3/4 × 6 × 57 1/2	B
1	3/4 × 2 3/4 × 57 1/2	D
1	3/4 × 5 × 48	C
2	1/4 × 29 3/4 × 80	to cover
5	1/8 × 1 × 6	hold-down
1	1 1/2 × 5	hasp
1 gross	# 7 1/2" fh	screw
1 gross	#4 3/8" rh	screw
24	#8 1 1/4" fh	screw
15	1/4" × 2"	bolts
360"	2" metal roof edge	
45 yd.	30" wide canvas	
2 lb.	Weldwood ext. glue	

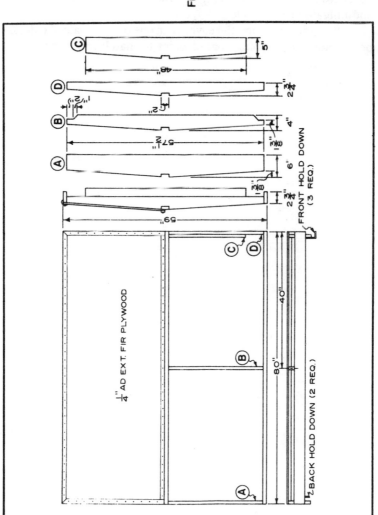

Fig. 7-8. Box cover dimensions.

123

all outside corners. This trim can be made in the metal shop with the use of the shear and bar-folder. Cover the plywood with glue and smooth canvas over it. Before glue is dry, place the metal edge in position and screw down with #4 3/8-inch rh wood screws at 6-inch intervals. Then screw the metal strip in place down the center of cover.

Make front hold-downs (three are required) from 1/8-×-1-×-6-inch metal scrap. Two straps of the same size are bolted to back of frame and fit in stake holes of truck bed to keep cover from sliding back. Next, bolt the lock hasp to back of cover and tailgate of the truck.

After prime painting the cover with one or two coats of exterior prime, add the finishing coat of paint to match the truck.

SPECIAL PAINTING TECHNIQUES

Have you considered a lesson on cobwebbing, lace, and freak drops? Don't laugh; these terms, and several others, refer to contemporary custom auto body spray painting techniques.

The phenomenon of special automobile finishes is not a new one. For many years, hot rods and custom show cars displayed very special finishes applied by painters who were well known for their customizing and painting skills. At first, their work consisted of many coats of lacquer with much hand rubbing between coats to increase the depth of the finish. Later, the customizers begin to develop special paints such as candy-apple, pearlescent, and metalflake. Automobiles finished with these paints were usually one uniform color.

Recently, a whole new concept in custom auto painting has emerged. The paints remain the same, but the spray painting techniques, such as cobwebbing, lace, and freak drops, are entirely new. The creative talents of these spray painters were recognized by one urban art museum which exhibited their handiwork on crash helmets and motorcycle gas tanks and fenders. Most of the best know custom auto sprayers have unique styles which are instantly recognizable by followers of this growing art form.

Terms Defined. Cobwebbing is a technique in which unthinned lacquer is shot at a slightly higher pressure than usual. This results in a "spray" that is actually a steady stream of stringy paint. The painter directs the thread-like stream over a panel, usually prepainted a contrasting color, in a random manner. When it is dry, the panel is wet-sanded smooth, and assumes a cobwebbish appearance.

Lace painting is a technique in which pieces of lace tablecloths or curtains are taped to a panel as stencils. The painter shoots over the lace, removes it, and rubs the paint down to produce an intricate pattern.

Freak drops are "splats" made by quick, short pulls of the spray gun trigger, much like the "blots" which are produced in most spray booths, but these are planned. As a finish for each of the above techniques, a protective coat of clear acrylic is sprayed over the special effect.

Other interesting custom spray painting designs and techniques include murals, shading, paneling, flames and scallops, fogging, smoke, imagineering, stencils, and ribbon painting. The exclusive use of any single technique usually results in ineffective, rather garish looking finishes. The imaginative blending of several techniques on a car, however, can produce a subtle, esthetic finish.

TRAILER WINCH

While welding is an ideal method of permanently joining parts in fabricating, and an excellent solution to the repair of broken metal objects, it also has an equally important place in manufacturing in the production of basic weldments.

Weldments and castings compete in the same general area. Each are primary products requiring additional machining for completion. As primary products, castings require the expense of patterns, the labor and facilities of a foundry, as well as a moderately high volume of production to amortize pattern costs. Weldments, on the other hand, can be built up from parts cut from individual layouts, by template guided torches, or by mechanized torches.

Figure 7-9 shows a boat-trailer winch using a typical weldment for the frame. Other weldments include the cable drum, the ratchet pawl, and the handle sleeve.

All parts were torch-cut from layout patterns, and the basic frame was completely built up before the bushing holes were line-bored. The drum offers considerable challenge to welding in a confined area while the tip of the ratchet pawl offers experience in surface buildup. The retaining washer in the handle sleeve is secured by a fillet of silver solder.

The winch was designed about a set of used automotive gears and a chain. The gears and chain are available at any auto salvage yard, and the only alteration of plans possibly necessary, due to different auto models, would be the gear end of the winch shafts. Chains can be shortened to suit the need. The winch makes an inexpensive welding project of considerable value in both learning experience and utility.

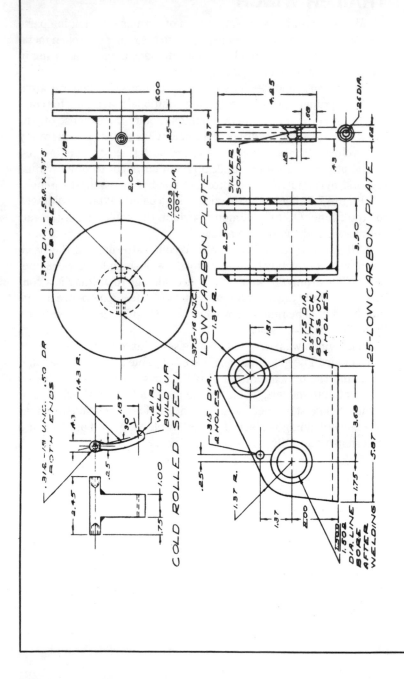

COLD ROLLED STEEL

LOW CARBON PLATE

.25-LOW CARBON PLATE

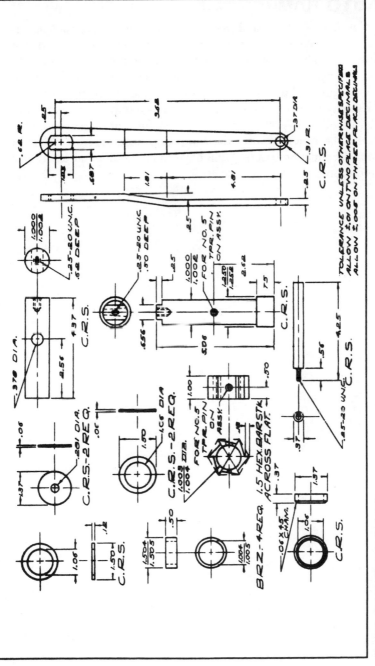

Fig. 7-9. Boat-trailer winch details.

AUTO RAMP

A metal-cutting band saw or reciprocating power hack saw is very desirable for this project, as there are many pieces to be cut (Fig. 7-10). Designing and building the jigs and/or fixtures is a very interesting phase of the project. They must be easy to use, maintain established dimensional tolerances, and be sturdy enough to survive the run. One of our jigs for a sub-assembly is a good example. It will do everything you could ask for, but the subassembly cannot be removed after the components are together. Most of your "production tooling" will have to be modified at least once before production is completed.

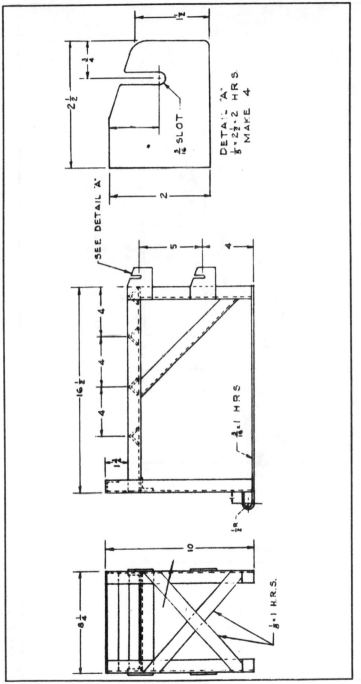

Fig. 7-10. Auto ramp construction details.

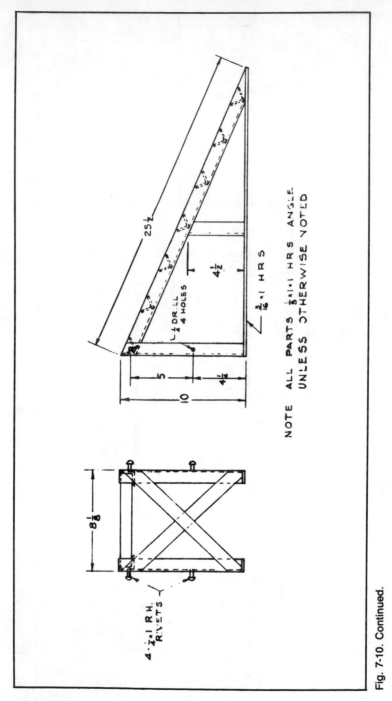

NOTE ALL PARTS $\frac{5}{8} \times 1$ HRS ANGLE
UNLESS OTHERWISE NOTED

Fig. 7-10. Continued.

132

WELDING BENCH

Anyone who has worked in a welding shop knows that it is difficult to find a good bench for cutting steel with an oxyacetylene cutting torch. All-steel benches are not satisfactory because they are affected by heat, and the grille work is easily cut. Benches of angle iron and pipe with welded joints are far more durable than steel benches. In addition, they have several modifications which make them more convenient to use.

First, place the brick around the outer edges of the top so that there is always a level place to rest your arm while cutting. A piece of plate laid over the brick produces a smoother surface. See Fig. 7-11.

The 1-inch grating can be purchased from most junk dealers. When it is severely burned and cut, you can remove and replace it without removing the brick.

Collect small pieces of steel and slag by placing a box under the table.

Finally, attach a chain to the side of the bench for a friction lighter, so that the lighter is always available for starting the cutting torch.

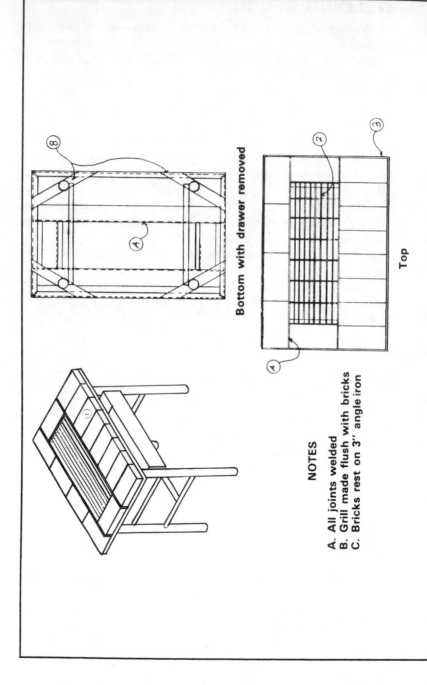

Bottom with drawer removed

Top

NOTES

A. All joints welded
B. Grill made flush with bricks
C. Bricks rest on 3" angle iron

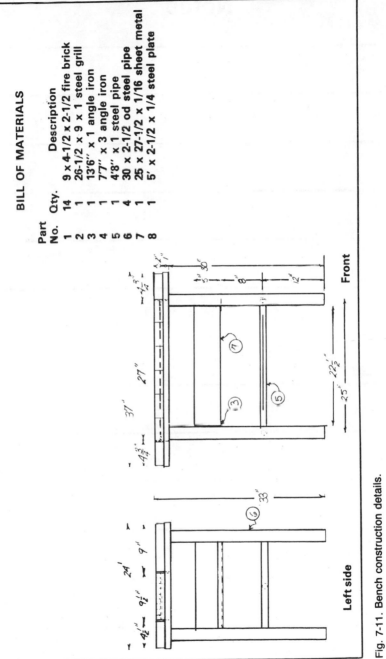

BILL OF MATERIALS

Part No.	Qty.	Description
1	14	9 x 4-1/2 x 2-1/2 fire brick
2	1	26-1/2 x 9 x 1 steel grill
3	1	13'6" x 1 angle iron
4	1	77" x 3 angle iron
5	1	4'8" x 1 steel pipe
6	4	30 x 2-1/2 od steel pipe
7	1	25 x 27-1/2 x 1/16 sheet metal
8	1	5' x 2-1/2 x 1/4 steel plate

Front

Left side

Fig. 7-11. Bench construction details.

Notes

Notes

Notes

Notes

Notes

Notes

Notes

Notes

Notes

Index

Index

Edited by Steven Bolt

Other Bestsellers From TAB

Other Bestsellers From TAB

☐ **TIME GATE: HURTLING BACKWARD THROUGH HISTORY—Pellegrino**

Taking a new approach to time travel, this totally fascinating history of life on Earth transports you backward from today's modern world through the very beginning of man's existence. Interwoven with stories and anecdotes, and illustrated with exceptional drawings and photographs, this is history as it should always have been written! It's a book that will have you spellbound from first page to last! Includes a foreword by noted science and science fiction author Isaac Asimov. 238 pp., 142 illus. Large Format (7″ × 10″).
Paper $16.95   Book No. 1863

☐ **VIDEO CASSETTE RECORDERS: BUYING, USING AND MAINTAINING**

Keep in step with the fast-paced world of home video recording! Find out about the newest equipment developments and recording techniques! Get practical tips on choosing the right video equipment for your own needs! Learn how to make your own professional-quality video productions! You'll find all the technical data you need on the components of a home recording system, and more! 156 pp., 41 illus.
**Paper $8.95   Hard $14.95
Book No. 1490**

☐ **LOCKS AND ALARMS —Allen**

A do-it-yourselfer's guide to installation, maintenance, and repair of locks, alarms, and complete home and auto security systems! Even rising crime rates and increased burglary statistics can't disturb your peace of mind and security when you know your home, family, and auto are properly protected against thieves, intruders, and other safety threats. And the reason you'll be sure you're adequately protected is because you'll have installed and checked your locks and security systems yourself . . . with the help of this excellent new guide. 352 pp., 327 illus.
**Paper $15.95   Hard $21.95
Book No. 1559**